A LOAF OF
BREAD

A LOAF OF BREAD

Bread in History, in the Kitchen,
and on the Table

GAIL DUFF

CHARTWELL
BOOKS, INC.

A QUARTO BOOK

Published by Chartwell Books
A division of Book Sales, Inc.
114 Northfield Avenue
Edison New Jersey 08837

This edition produced for sale in the U.S.A. and its territories and dependencies only.

ISBN 0-7858-1012-9
This book was designed and produced by
Quarto Publishing plc
The Old Brewery
6 Blundell St
London N7 9BH

Art editor: Sally Bond
Designer: Liz Brown
Editor: Nancy Terry
Copy editor: Madelaine Weston, Beverly Le Blanc
Managing editor: Sally MacEachern
Picture researcher: Zoe Holtermann
Photographer: Iain Bagwell, Colin Bowling
Illustrator: Jane Smith
Home Economist: Gail Duff
Stylist: Rachel Jukes
Assistant art director: Penny Cobb
Art director: Moira Clinch
Editorial director: Pippa Rubinstein

Typeset in Great Britain by Central Southern Typesetters, Eastbourne
Manufactured in Hong Kong by Regent Publishing Services Ltd
Printed in Singapore by Star Standard Industries (Pte) Ltd

CONTENTS

INTRODUCTION

THERE ARE FEW THINGS IN THE WORLD SO SATISFYING AS BREAD. IT HAS BEEN A STAPLE FOOD IN MANY COUNTRIES FOR THOUSANDS OF YEARS AND IT WILL PROBABLY BE SO FOR THOUSANDS MORE. THE SMELL OF BAKING BREAD IS ONE OF THE MOST ENTICING SCENTS IN THE WORLD.

Demeter, seen here with her sickle and sheaf of wheat and poppies, was the Greek goddess of the harvest. In rescuing Persephone from the underworld, she guaranteed spring would always return after winter.

Early settlers found it difficult to grow European varieties of wheat. Today, the United States is one of the biggest grain producers in the world.

Bread has been so important to human existence that, in the Bible and in many classical stories, the word itself is often synonymous with "food." In most English-speaking countries, "bread" and "dough" are colloquial expressions for money.

Because in early history bread was literally the "staff of life," it is at the center of many religious customs and festivals. In some parts of the world, a goddess or god, or the giver and taker away of life, was associated with corn, because people's very existence depended on this grain. The Aztecs worshiped a corn god, and in ancient Greece, Demeter was the goddess of the harvest and her daughter, Persephone, the corn maiden. In other countries, planting, growth, and harvesting of grain represented the continuing cycle of birth, life, and death. Even now, there is still a certain magic about the life cycle of the crop. Plowing opens up welcoming tracts of earth, ready to receive the seed. Gradually the earth is covered in green as the young stalks grow. When the grain is mature, the landscape turns golden, the harvesting starts, and the age-old process begins again.

Whatever the country or the religious beliefs, there was always great celebration when the harvest was safely gathered. It was the culmination of a year's hard work, plowing, sowing, and reaping, and often provided reassurance that a community would survive the coming winter. Worldwide, people still celebrate the safe gathering of the harvest.

Depending on the types of grain grown, every country has its preferences for different types of flour and different baking methods, born of long historical associations and climatic differences. Corn bread, for example, was first made by Native Americans and unknown to the first European settlers, who continued to stoically plant their seed corn before discovering that the native corn thrived better than the imported cereal crops. Bannocks and oatcakes became popular in Scotland because they were easy to make on flat stones or iron griddles in cottages with open fires but not ovens.

Bread and cheese, chapatis and lentils, tortillas and beans, bagels and smoked fish are classic combinations, born of different climates, styles of farming, and ways of life. Almost every

6

country in the world has its own classic bread recipe, often created in homes and eaten locally at first, but later taken across continents by travelers to become internationally known and commercially available.

When you eat bread you are taking part in a cycle that begins with sowing the seed and ends with loaves being sold. You may not feel a connection with the farming end of bread production, but you can still take part in the cycle by buying the flour and making your own bread. In doing so, you will be carrying on a skill that has been practiced for millennia. You, too, can experience the feel of the dough in your hands, the pleasure when the dough begins to rise, the tantalizing smell as the loaves bake, and the satisfaction in seeing your family and friends happy and well-fed.

Making bread is special. With a few simple ingredients and a dollop of enthusiasm, you end up with a beautiful, sweet-smelling, delicious

Instant Bread

Making bread by hand can be very satisfying, but if you are in a hurry or short of time, a bread-making machine is a welcome addition to your kitchen. Just put the ingredients in the machine, select a setting, and then walk away until it is time to open the machine and take out the loaf. Depending on your machine, you should be able to make yeasted and non-yeasted breads, and also to adapt conventional bread recipes. Consult the instruction booklet that comes with the machine, or contact the 800 help line provided by the company if you have any queries.

Special harvest loaves are baked all over the world. Many are used to decorate places of worship at services where thanks is given for a successful harvest.

food that will not only provide you with energy, vitamins, and minerals, but also will be an easy accompaniment to other foods.

Making bread is not difficult. All you need are a few basic ingredients and the patience to wait for the dough to rise. You don't need expensive equipment, and for some recipes you don't even need an oven. It doesn't have to be time-consuming either. You can use a bread machine if you are in a particular hurry, either to make the entire loaf or just to knead the bread. Even if you stick entirely to traditional methods, you can leave the dough to rise for an hour, after the initial mixing and kneading before shaping it.

When you are making bread for the first time, start with the basic recipe (page 30). Once you have mastered it, experiment by changing the type of flour or try different yeasts to see which one suits you best. Experiment with shapes and sizes of loaves. Soon, you will have a customized bread recipe that suits your oven, your available ingredients, and your taste. Then you can confidently move onto the recipes in the book with more ingredients or more complicated methods.

7

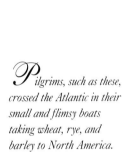

Pilgrims, such as these, crossed the Atlantic in their small and flimsy boats taking wheat, rye, and barley to North America.

THE HISTORY OF BREAD

THROUGHOUT MUCH OF THE WORLD, THE DEVELOPMENT OF BREAD AND THE RISE OF CIVILIZATIONS HAVE GONE HAND-IN-HAND. WHERE MANY SOCIETIES WERE ESTABLISHED, GRAIN WAS GROWN AND WHEREVER THESE PEOPLE HAVE TRAVELED, THE KNOWLEDGE OF GROWING GRAIN AND BAKING BREAD HAS GONE WITH THEM AND CONTRIBUTED TO THEIR SURVIVAL IN NEW LANDS.

The ancient Egyptians grew corn in the fertile land around the Nile Delta. Their planting and harvesting techniques were unchanged for centuries.

The seeds of wild grasses were first recognized as a nutritious food around 10 000 B.C., when people lived by hunting and gathering. This happened more or less simultaneously in Europe and the Middle East and also on the plains of what is now the United States.

In the region of the Andes, an ancestor of corn was gathered alongside wild tomatoes and potatoes. In different parts of the world, grains were ground with stones and mixed with water, and eaten as a kind of porridge.

Around 9000 B.C. permanent settlements were established on the grassy areas of the Middle East, and people first learned if some seed were retained from the grain harvest and re-sown, a more regular supply of food could be guaranteed. With the development of settled— as opposed to nomadic—living, people had more time to experiment and it was discovered the porridge mixture could be cooked in small amounts on hot, flat stones to make small cakes of unleavened bread. These were the ancestors of all the flat breads we know today, such as tortillas, chapatis, and Ethiopian *injera*.

Around 6000 B.C. bread-making wheats with larger grains and, eventually, a high gluten content were developed. Their use soon spread,

Fannie Merritt Farmer

Miss Fannie Merritt Farmer was born in the eastern United States around the middle of the nineteenth century. For some years she ran the Boston Cookery School, where she taught young women how to make all the classic American dishes, such as pumpkin pie, chowder, planked steak, and a boiled dinner. Her book, The Original Boston Cooking School Cookbook, *was first published in 1896, and it was full of the basic recipes and common sense that had made her school so popular. By the time she died in 1915, her book had sold six million copies and the name Fannie Farmer had become synonymous with good cooking and good housewifery.*

Fannie Farmer's chapter on "Bread and Bread-making" includes details about types of wheat, milling, flour, and leavening agents, together with the basic principles for making an excellent loaf, all of which are still relevant today.

"The study of bread-making," she wrote, "is of no slight importance, and deserves more attention than it receives. Considering its great value, it seems unnecessary and wrong to find poor bread on the table."

Eliza Acton

In nineteenth-century England, particularly around the 1850s, the price and availability of wheat for bread making varied tremendously. As a result, bakers commonly adulterated flour—or in their terms, "improved" it—with such ingredients as potatoes, alum, chalk, and bonemeal, which could both bulk out the flour and improve the appearance of an inferior loaf.

Conditions in many bakeries were far from hygienic, and there are shocking descriptions of flour being kept in the damp, "and, above all, sickly, perspiring men in contact with our food."

All this so appalled English cook Eliza Acton that, in 1857, she was moved to write The English Bread Book, *exposing the tricks and bad practices of the bakery trade, and urging all housewives to bake their own bread.*

She gives details of flours, raising agents, and methods, recipes such as "Excellent Suffolk Bread," "Good Family Bread," and "The Frugal Housewife's Brown Bread," and tips such as "The Tests of Well-Made Bread." All the instructions are clear and concise and apply just as much today as when they were first written.

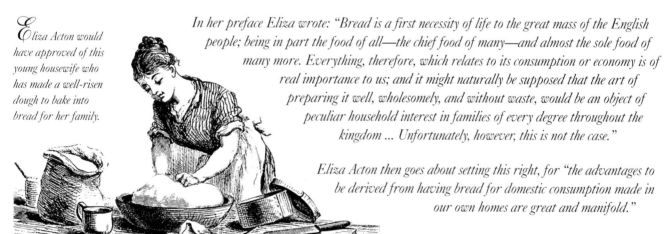

Eliza Acton would have approved of this young housewife who has made a well-risen dough to bake into bread for her family.

In her preface Eliza wrote: "Bread is a first necessity of life to the great mass of the English people; being in part the food of all—the chief food of many—and almost the sole food of many more. Everything, therefore, which relates to its consumption or economy is of real importance to us; and it might naturally be supposed that the art of preparing it well, wholesomely, and without waste, would be an object of peculiar household interest in families of every degree throughout the kingdom ... Unfortunately, however, this is not the case."

Eliza Acton then goes about setting this right, for "the advantages to be derived from having bread for domestic consumption made in our own homes are great and manifold."

9

people were better fed and the early civilizations began to develop. Then, by trial and error, it was learned that a dough left for a long time in a warm place would start to ferment and that process made the finished result more palatable. This must have been the way sourdough breads originated.

It was the Egyptians who first discovered and developed the use of yeast, giving rise to the breads we know today. The Greeks called the Egyptians *artophagoi*, meaning "the bread eaters," and part of the wages of the Egyptian troops was 4 pounds of wheat and barley bread per day. However, only the rich were able to eat yeasted bread and even this was never perfect. One of the Pharaohs hanged his baker because of the poor quality of his loaves.

In remote places such as the Isle of Skye in Scotland, where there were no stores and few local mills, wheat for bread making had to be ground at home. These nineteenth-century crofters are shown using a hand mill.

In ancient settlements, such as this one on the west coast of Ireland, small, flat cakes made of mixed grains and seeds would have been baked on hot stones by the fire.

By about 1000 B.C. in ancient Greece, it seems barley was the most popular grain for making bread, but by 450 B.C. wheat was the staple grain. Bread was raised by keeping a batch of dough from the last baking to start the next, and rich people were able to add honey, milk, pepper, and sweet wine to the dough to vary the textures and flavors.

At the same time, different types of wheat and barley were being developed in Britain and western Europe. Small hearth-cakes found in Glastonbury, England, dating from 1 B.C., contain wheat, barley, wild oats, and the seeds of a wild plant called *orache*.

The first domed ovens were used in Europe during the Iron Age. Yeast from brewing beer was used for the dough, producing breads more like those of today.

For a long time, the Romans preferred a thick porridge called *puls* to bread. Eventually they took to baking, but they are reputed to have been bad at it. Early Roman bread was difficult to digest, but, toward the end of the Roman era, the rich demanded fine white bread, thus establishing an attitude that was to last for almost 1,000 years: white bread was for the wealthy and whole-wheat for the poor.

In Saxon times in Britain, bread made from a mixture of wheat and rye, called *maslin* bread, was the most common. Made at home, it was usually unleavened and baked on a hearth stone. There were, however, professional bakers who made leavened bread.

In medieval times, all over Europe, the poor used what grains they could get, together with weed seeds, ground beans or chestnuts, and even, in some places, ground tree bark, while the rich demanded the whitest bread possible. By the fourteenth and fifteenth centuries there were many types of bread available, including those enriched with butter, milk, and eggs. There were also a number of laws and regulations governing quality. In sixteenth-century Europe, better-quality grains were favored in different areas, so fewer of the bulking ingredients had to be used. Bread was getting better.

At the end of the fifteenth century, Christopher Columbus found corn in what is now Cuba and took seeds back to Spain. He also found tribes in the Bahamas making bread from the fermented seeds of the zamia plant. The Spanish discovered cassava bread in the same area and took the plant to Africa, where it soon became a staple food. When Cortez invaded Mexico, the Spaniards planted wheat, and a colony established by Walter Raleigh first grew wheat in North Carolina in 1585.

From the seventeenth century onward, wheat growing, milling, and baking improved on both sides of the Atlantic, and breads and methods were devised to suit the new conditions. American settlers learned how to make corn breads; trekkers in South Africa devised a way of baking in cast-iron pots.

During the nineteenth century, greater quantities of commercial bread were being made and bread was often adulterated with ingredients such as chalk and bonemeal. This caused Fannie Farmer in America and Eliza Acton and William Cobbett in England to speak out for home baking.

In 1856, John Dauglish, an English chemist, found a method for aerating bread dough, but bakers were reluctant to use the idea until 1900.

The twentieth century has seen a rise in the status and quality of bread. For many years

In the Middle Ages, plowing and sowing had changed very little since Egyptian times. Wooden plows were drawn across the fields by horses and the seed was sown by hand. Harvesting was done with sickles.

In fourteenth-century England, a baker who made underweight loaves was punished by being drawn through the streets with a loaf around his neck, and was then placed in the pillory.

white, sliced bread was the most popular. It was new, convenient, and reasonably priced. Everyone could now have pure white bread. Then, in the 1960s, it was discovered white may not be the healthiest option and whole-wheat bread became fashionable because of its additional fiber and, for a while, was more expensive than white bread.

Approaching the next millennium, we now have the perfect situation. In many countries, bread is reasonably priced and well made and there is a choice of varieties. It is now often easy to find Italian ciabatta, Indian nan, French baguettes, Scandinavian pumpernickel, and English muffins. Some are whole-wheat, some white, and some are a mixture. Bread has become extremely cosmopolitan.

A large proportion of the bread bought today is made in factories. This produces loaves of an even size, weight, and texture, but many people prefer handmade bread.

William Cobbett

William Cobbett, 1762–1835, is now best known for his book Rural Rides, *in which he described his journeys through eighteenth-century England, but during his lifetime he was probably best known for his* Cottage Economy, *which, soon after it was published in 1823, found its way into many country kitchens.*

It was a book full of information for "cottagers" who kept their own cows, pigs, sheep, and goats, brewed their own beer, and made their own bread. It was his view everybody should be as self-sufficient as possible, which would add to their own prosperity and contentment and to the eventual prosperity of the country.

William Cobbett was much concerned about the adulteration of bread in commercial bakeries and the price of the loaves in the stores, so did all he could to promote home baking:

"How wasteful, then, and, indeed, how shameful, for a labourer's wife to go into a baker's shop; and how negligent, how criminally careless of the welfare of his family, must the labourer be, who permits so scandalous a use of the proceeds of his labour! … As to the act of making bread, it would be shocking indeed, if that had to be taught by the means of books. Every woman, high or low, ought to know how to make bread."

He nevertheless goes on to describe the bread-making process. "And what is the result? Why, good, wholesome food, sufficient for a considerable family for a week, prepared in three or four hours."

11

FOLKLORE AND FESTIVALS

ALL OVER THE WORLD, BREAD IS SUCH A BASIC NECESSITY OF HUMAN LIFE THERE IS PROBABLY MORE FOLKLORE RELATED TO IT THAN TO ALMOST ANY OTHER FOOD.

The many harvest customs around the world date back to early times when corn was cut by hand.

The harvest festival is a service in which thanks are given for a good crop, safely gathered in to provide food for the coming year.

The beginnings of ritual, tradition, and religion are strongly linked to the baking of bread. Rituals and ceremonies developed to bring luck to the harvest and to make sure it was plentiful for the winter.

HARVEST FESTIVALS

Since wheat was first grown, about 9000 B.C., a successful harvest has meant the culmination of a year's labor and the supply of a store of food for the months ahead—a time of celebration.

In pre-Christian times, the first day of the harvest was around August 1, on the Celtic festival of Lughnasagh, the day of the sun god Lugh, and loaves baked on this day were offered to him in thanks. The day was later absorbed into the Christian tradition to become the Saxon *lafmass* ("loaf mass"); this later became the festival of Lammas, when loaves baked with wheat from the first harvest were taken to church to be blessed. In England in the 1980s, bakers introduced a Lammas loaf race, in which they competed to see who could cut the wheat, grind it, and produce loaves in the shortest time.

Before the days of the combine harvester, western European countries had many "last load" customs. The last sheaf to be cut was thought to be where the corn spirit, who lived in the fields, had taken refuge. In some places, it was thought unlucky to be the person who cut the sheaf, so the harvesters threw their sickles at it from a distance. In other places, it was the task of a young girl of the village to cut the sheaf, and she become the "Harvest Queen." The sheaf was garlanded with ribbons and flowers and taken back to the farm on a decorated cart, pulled by two horses, and the harvest was declared complete. In Sussex, England, the cry was:

> *We've ploughed,*
> *We've sowed,*
> *We've reaped,*
> *We've mowed,*
> *We've carried our last load*
> *And aren't overthrowed!*

Then it was back to the barn for the harvest supper where, in pride of place, there was a loaf baked in the shape of a wheatsheaf. This same wheatsheaf loaf is still baked for harvest celebrations in parts of Europe. It can be seen in bakery windows and as part of church decorations for annual harvest festivals.

BREAD SHAPES

Almost every country has its own traditional shapes. Many of the shapes have origins and meanings that go back for many thousands of years. In Germany these breads are called *Gebiltbrote*, or "picture breads." Many shapes have pagan origins, while others have Christian significance. Both Germany and Switzerland have more than 200 different bread shapes.

Braided breads are made in many countries, and it is said they go back to the time when widows sacrificed their hair following the death of a husband. In the same way, breads in the shape of farm animals replaced the yearly animal sacrifices to the gods.

Loaves in the shape of a sun, or marked with a star or wheel pattern, were used as sun symbols to honor the sun god at midsummer and Beltane (May Day). In some places they were rolled down hills, and in others placed at altars or ritually eaten. An equal-sided cross was added before it was used on hot-cross buns in Christian England during Lent or at Easter. The German pretzel was a moon symbol in honor of the moon goddess.

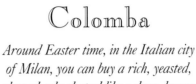

Crowns play a significant part in Eastern European weddings. This one is taking place in Russia.

Colomba

Around Easter time, in the Italian city of Milan, you can buy a rich, yeasted, almond cake shaped like a dove, known as colomba. *Milan is in Lombardy, where there are rich pasture lands, so the dough for the cake is made with butter and eggs.*

The custom of making colomba *goes back to the Easter of 1176, when the Milanese army was lined up with the rest of the forces of the Lombard League ready to fight for Pope Alexander III against the soldiers of the Holy Roman Empire. Two doves flew down and settled on the Milanese standards. The Milanese saw this as a symbol of divine protection. It encouraged them in the battle and they defeated the emperor's army.*

The anniversary of the battle is still commemorated in the Church of San Simpliciano in Milan, where a special mass is said and two doves are released from the altar.

Some harvest customs were designed not only to give thanks for the year's crop, but also to guarantee plenty of corn, and therefore bread, in the year to come.

A CALENDAR OF BREAD

The following celebrations can give only an idea of the extent to which bread plays a part in rituals and festivals.

NEW YEAR

In one area of Switzerland, children who make lanterns for the New Year procession are given a small loaf called an *Altjahrman* ("old year man").

In the Ukraine, small sourdough rolls called *balabushky* are baked on New Year's Eve. One contains a coin and it is said that the girl who finds it will be married within the year.

In Greece, a New Year yeast cake, baked in a round container and sprinkled with sesame seeds, is cut by the head of the family when the family members have all returned from church on New Year's Eve or New Year's morning.

TWELFTH NIGHT

In Spain, the three kings, *Los Reyes Majors*, arrive by camel from Bethlehem on the night of January 6, bringing gifts, and the *roscon de reyes*, or "three kings' cake," is baked. It is a rich yeast cake decorated with frosting and candied peel, and often a trinket is baked inside, to bring good fortune to the person who receives it.

In Mexico, there is a *rosca de los reyes*. The one to find the favor in the bread must give a party on February 2.

SHROVE TUESDAY AND ASH WEDNESDAY

Shrove Tuesday buns called *semlor* are baked in Sweden. They are small, round, and sweet, filled with almond paste and served in a bowl of hot milk and cinnamon.

A pre-Lent ceremony still observed in Russia features a young girl dressed as Spring being offered ceremonial bread and salt as a welcoming gift, while a man dressed as Winter receives a pitcher of wine as a farewell.

LENT

Apprentices of the Guild of Bakers in Switzerland finish their training in Lent by making *lochli brot* ("hole-y bread").

In Turkey, Greece, Armenia, and Cyprus, a rolled bread filled with olives was traditionally eaten during Lent to add flavor to a diet in which meat, eggs, and dairy products were forbidden for 40 days.

PALM SUNDAY

In Mexico, Holy Week Bread, consisting of small rolls, is taken to church in a basket, together with medicinal herbs, local wine, and sometimes money, as an offering to the poor.

GOOD FRIDAY

Small, sweet fruit buns with a cross on top, called hot cross buns, are baked in England on Good Friday. It was once believed buns baked on that day would never become moldy. They were nailed to the ceilings of houses and bakeries as a protection from fire. They were also kept to be used, crumbled into water, as a medicine for a number of ills.

In Russia, however, it was thought unlucky to bake on Good Friday and if you did, the baked bread would turn into wood.

In Gundelmontag, Switzerland, a large loaf, with a head molded on it, is impaled on a pole and paraded around the town. Touching the head is supposed to bring good luck.

In Greece, the tsoureke, *a loaf baked with a colored egg in the middle, is an esssential part of Easter celebrations.*

EASTER

In Estonia, Latvia, and Lithuania *kulich*, a loaf made from circles of spiced dough baked in a pyramid shape, is a key part of the Easter meal.

In Greece, the Lenten fast ends with *tsoureke*, bread made from a rich dough coiled around a red-colored hard-boiled egg.

HARVEST

One of the most spectacular of harvest festivals is the *Tabuleiros*, in Tomar, Portugal. Every year, 15 young girls are chosen to carry the *tabuleiro*, or "tray," of bread in procession. The tray, in the form of a crown of bread rolls, is worn on the head and is often built up to be as tall as the wearer and decorated with sprigs of wheat and paper flowers. Because each one weighs about 26 pounds, the girls are helped by male relatives. In the evening, oxen are killed and people are blessed at the Church of St. John the Baptist. The next day there are bullfights, dancing, and fireworks, and meat, wine, and bread are given to the poor. The festival originated to honor the Roman goddess Ceres to offer thanks for a good and plentiful harvest, but is now a Christian celebration.

At the festival of Tabuleiros *in Portugal, the young girls of the village of Tomar dress in white and wear crowns of bread. These girls are wearing the traditional costume of the area.*

THE DAY OF THE DEAD (*NOVEMBER 1 AND 2*)

This festival, held to honor ancestors, takes place in Mexico. The special bread can be made in human, animal, or plant shapes, or round, and is decorated with skulls, bones, and tears of dough.

ST. NICHOLAS' DAY (*DECEMBER 6*)

In Switzerland, various shaped breads, in the form of religious symbols and characters, are made for this day.

ST. LUCIA'S DAY (*DECEMBER 13*)

This festival is celebrated in Sweden. Early in the morning, the daughter of the house is dressed in white, with a wreath of greenery and lighted candles on her head, to offer the rest of the household a plate of saffron buns. The buns are made in various animal shapes, and the most popular are the *lussekatter,* or cat's face.

Decorated gingerbread, in many different shapes, is popular at Christmastime in Germany.

CHRISTMAS

In Verona, Italy, *pan doro* (golden bread) is baked. It is rich with eggs and butter, baked in a star-shape, and strewn with confectioners' sugar.

Germany's main Christmas bread is *Dresdner stollen,* a rich fruit bread, packed with dried fruits, candied peel, and slivered almonds, baked in a long shape and dredged with confectioners' sugar.

Scandinavian Christmas breads reflect the old Yule festivals marking the winter solstice. Animal-shaped loaves, harking back to the animal sacrifices, are still very popular. A Christmas bread made from piecrust dough, known as *Julekage,* is popular throughout the whole of Denmark.

Sweden has two Christmas breads. *Dopbrod* ("dipping bread"), made with rye flour and flavored with fennel and anise seeds, is made both commercially and at home to dip into the Christmas Eve ham soup. *Prastens har* ("priest's hair") made from white bread dough, is shaped like a wig with curls and decorated with dried and candied fruits. Although the name and shape of the wig date from the seventeenth century, it is thought that the tradition is pre-Christian in origin.

15

In Mexico, the Day of the Dead festival is a time to honor and remember members of the family who have died. Candles are lit at dusk in their memory and special breads, decorated with skulls, bones, and tears of dough, are baked.

BREADS AROUND THE WORLD

EVERY COUNTRY HAS ITS OWN CHARACTERISTIC BREADS. SOME BREADS ARE BAKED FOR FESTIVALS AND FOR SPECIAL OCCASIONS, BUT MANY ARE REGIONAL OR NATIONAL FAVORITES BAKED EVERY DAY. SOME ARE SERVED ALONGSIDE OTHER DISHES, SOME ARE ACCOMPANIMENT AND EATING UTENSIL IN ONE, SOME ARE MEALS IN THEMSELVES AND OTHERS ARE SWEET TREATS.

UNITED STATES

Bread in the United States is the result of many influences, including Native American customs, frontier needs, and the importation of ethnic specialties from around the world. A variety of corn breads (see pages 102-3) are still made, particularly in the South, and corn is also an ingredient in the steamed brown breads of New England, also often made with a mixture of flours. Early pioneers developed different sourdough bread recipes and salt risin' breads, that are still popular. In the north of the country and into Canada, bannocks, cooked over the fire on a flat pan, were food for trappers. Doughnuts came from the same area. In the East, more sophisticated types of bread were developed, such as Parker House rolls and Philadelphia sticky buns. Immigrants coming to America brought their own specialties. Jewish bagels, for example, came originally from Austria, and the inspiration for muffins came from England.

Something tasty contained in bread always makes a hearty snack. Hot dogs are now a popular snack worldwide.

16

CENTRAL AND SOUTH AMERICA

The grain indigenous to the countries in this area is corn, which is used to make the thin, flat breads called tortillas served with every meal in Mexico. Tortillas can also be deep-fried, either whole or in wedges, to make *tostadas* and *tostaditas*. The Spaniards introduced wheat to Mexico and it was soon adopted by the local people. South Americans like sweet foods and many of the breads and rolls there contain a small amount of sugar.

THE WEST INDIES

Originating in the West Indies was cassava bread, which is still popular. It has an earthy flavor and can be eaten plain or fried. Corn is also indigenous to the area and corn breads are still popular. Wheat was taken to the West Indies by the first European settlers and today it is made into tin loaves, flat breads, and rolls. Deep-fried pieces of plain dough called "floats" are a popular carry-out snack in Trinidad. All over the West Indies there is a taste for sweet breads, containing ingredients such as bananas, limes, coconut, nuts, and spices.

THE MIDDLE EAST

Wheat was first grown around the Middle East, where it has remained the staple grain used in hundreds of different breads. Widespread is *lavash*, a thin, slightly crisp bread baked in ovals and rounds in a clay oven called a *tonir*. Other flat breads include pita bread from Greece,

In Mexico, the tortilla is the staple bread, and many housewives still make them by hand in the traditional manner. The shaping and rolling process shown in this nineteenth-century print is exactly the same today.

mannaeesh from the Lebanon, *khobz-el-saluf* from the Yemen (both topped with herbs), and *barbari* from Iran. In Egypt, bread rings coated with sesame seeds are sold in the streets. Israel has bagels and also *cholla*, a rich, braided bread made for the Jewish Sabbath.

SOUTH AFRICA

When the first Europeans arrived in South Africa, they had to devise ways of making bread without raising agents and without conventional ovens. They developed various sourdough breads and a salt-rising bread very similar to the American ones. They also made small, hard rusks that would keep well on long journeys. *Mos*, made by fermenting raisins in water, was used as a starter for small, sweet buns. Bread was variously baked on a griddle or in a cast-iron pot, and pieces of dough were deep-fried to make *vetkoek* and *koeksisters* (see pages 118–19).

INDIA

Flatbreads are characteristic of India. The best known is chapati, made with a simple mixture of finely ground whole-wheat flour, water, and a little salt. A smaller, thicker variation is made from *gram* (chick-pea) flour, often flavored with coriander and chili. There is also *roti*, made with chapati dough but fried so it puffs up. *Puris* are a deep-fried variation. More substantial and thicker again are *parathas*, which are enriched with *ghee*, similar to clarified butter.

CHINA

Although China is more often associated with rice or noodles, it still has some bread recipes, mainly from the north of the country. The dough is often steamed to keep it white and glossy. Most popular are the flower rolls, which are shaped by a sharp knife and a chopstick into elaborate spirals. Dim sum from Canton are steamed bun snacks with sweet or savory fillings. The traditional accompaniment to Peking Duck is mandarin pancakes.

AUSTRALIA AND NEW ZEALAND

The first bread made by settlers in Australia was a round, unleavened loaf called a damper, baked in the ashes of a campfire. It was originally made from plain flour and water, and extras such as salt and powdered milk were added when and if available. Today, health breads have come to the fore. The most popular recipes for home baking are quick and easy, sweet, teatime treats.

Wheat was first grown in New Zealand in the early 1800s. It was quickly adopted by the Maori people, who devised a sourdough loaf, baked in a covered dish, called *rewena paraoa*. Nowadays, whole-wheat and mixed-grain breads are very popular in New Zealand.

GREAT BRITAIN

The breads of Great Britain range from simple, griddle-cooked oatcakes to rich, yeasted buns and cakes. The griddle, or girdle, was once common to the British household, and oatcakes and bannocks, Welsh cakes, Northumbrian singin' hinny, muffins, pikelets, and crumpets were produced on it. Most bread is made from wheat, and the most popular has always been white. Loaves are baked different shapes, including the large, oval bloomer and pan loaves.

In the Middle East, freshly made flat breads, baked in a tandoor oven, can be bought in local outdoor markets.

17

Proverb from Afar

Better beans and corn bread at home than cake and wine in the land of strangers.

GEORGIAN SAYING. (GEORGIA WAS FORMERLY PART OF THE SOVIET UNION.)

Rich, sweet breads, such as the Scots black bun, West Country saffron cakes, *bara brith* from Wales, and dough cake (see page 74) are still popular. The specialty of Northern Ireland (and indeed of the Irish Republic) is soda bread, which is widely available in both white or whole-wheat types.

FRANCE

The long, white baguette is the most recognizable of French breads, but there are many others. Some are made with the same dough, differently shaped, and others are made with different flours or by using different methods. The French make superb rich breads. The Brioche (see page 58) is light and golden and can be made plain or filled, and the flaky Croissant (see page 60) has become a favorite breakfast food throughout the world.

GERMANY AND AUSTRIA

There are countless varieties of bread produced in hundreds of different shapes. Rye and whole-wheat flours are popular, as are sourdough breads. These can be plain or flavored with onion or caraway seeds. The everyday bread of Germany is *Landbrot*. Usually made from rye

With a good supply of bread, the whole family will be kept well-fed and happy. A smiling housewife from Tuscany, in Italy, shows off her freshly baked loaves.

18

The Boulangerie

In France, very little bread is baked at home. There is a baker in every community and French housewives shop for bread daily.

The boulangerie, *or bread store, is open even on a Sunday morning, and sometimes all day Sunday if it is combined with a* patisserie *(a section of the store selling sweet pastries and cakes). Where there are several bakers in a community, they may stagger their working hours to fit in with each other and to keep their customers supplied. A* boulangerie *is often connected to a working bakery producing fresh bread two or even three times a day.*

The proliferation of local bakers, rather than large, central bakeries producing sliced, wrapped loaves, guarantees a wide variety of bread is available throughout France. Besides the classic French baguette, boulangeries *often sell up to 25 different types of bread, including regional specialties, many of which are peculiar to a small locality only. This turns shopping for bread in France into a culinary adventure.*

The Panetteria and the Forno

In Italy, every town or village has its own baker. In a large town or city it is referred to as a panetteria, *and in the smaller towns and villages as the* forno.

The panetteria *often has shelving and counters, and the windows display elaborate scenes of castles, farms, or palaces all made from bread. It sells many different kinds of rich and specialty breads, such as focaccia, pizza,* panettoni, *and even the French brioche.*

The forno *in a country village is often indistinguishable from an ordinary house. The whole process of baking and selling may take place in one room, or, if the building is larger, the oven may be situated in a room behind the store. Loaves are baked several times a day and taken straight from the oven to the store shelves. There is less variety than in the* panetteria *in the town, but the quality is always excellent.*

In the days when few, if any, of the village people had ovens in their own houses, pies, cakes, and homemade breads were taken to the forno *for communal baking in the brick oven.*

flour, it has a dark, crispy crust and a light brown crumb. White flour is made into shaped breads and also into small, crusty rolls. Pretzels, made in twisted knot shapes, are a tasty snack.

Austria is justly famous for its rich, sweet breads such as *kugelhupf* (see page 62).

ITALY

There are many regional breads in Italy. In the northernmost region, hearty bread made from rye flour is eaten with main meals and soups, but wheat flour is used everywhere else. There are flatbreads, such as focaccia and pizza, and small, crispy breadsticks. The newest plain bread is the ciabatta, made with a long rising method to give a slightly sour flavor. Sweet specialties are *Panettoni* (see page 69), *Colomba* (see page 13), and the Christmas bread *pan doro*.

SCANDINAVIA

Throughout Scandinavia, rye is the most widely used grain for everyday breads and crispbreads which are made both with yeast and sourdough. Plain white bread is not frequently eaten and it is often referred to as "French bread." However, enriched white breads such as *pulla*, a braided wreath made for Christmas, or the many versions of Danish pastry, are very popular.

The Galatea Tower in Figueres, Spain, has red walls decorated with bread.

19

SPAIN

Spanish bread is often baked in large loaves with a crisp crust and a soft crumb. White wheat flour is used throughout Spain, and loaf shapes vary from region to region. In tapas bars you may find a bread snack called *la pringa*, made from small buns topped with a spiced pork filling. The New Year specialty is *roscon de reyes*.

FLOURS

THE MAIN INGREDIENT OF ALL BREADS IS FLOUR, WHICH IS PRODUCED BY MILLING VARIOUS TYPES OF GRAIN. IT COMES IN MANY DIFFERENT GRADES OF COARSENESS AND IN COLORS RANGING FROM PURE WHITE, THROUGH YELLOW, TO DARK BROWN. ALTHOUGH THERE IS A WIDE VARIETY OF FLOURS AVAILABLE, EACH COUNTRY HAS ITS FAVORITE.

TYPES OF GRAIN

Wheat is the grain most commonly used to make bread throughout the world. Rye has a stronger flavor and darker color, and is very popular in certain European countries and in parts of North America. Flours from oats and barley can also be made into bread, but are more often used in mixtures of different types of flour rather than alone. Corn is used alone or in mixtures to make a variety of breads. The seeds of the buckwheat plant are also ground to make flour, traditionally used to make blinis.

THE STRUCTURE OF GRAIN

A cereal grain is made up of three basic parts: the husk or bran, which makes up the outer coating; the endosperm, which makes up the bulk of the grain; and the germ, which is the small section at the base of the grain from which, if the grain were planted, the plant would grow. The husk has little nutritional value in terms of vitamins or minerals, but it can be an important source of dietary fiber. The endosperm makes up about 80 percent of the grain and contains starch and proteins. The germ is rich in natural oil, iron, protein, and vitamins B and E.

MILLING

Whole-grain flours are made by milling the husk, endosperm, and germ together. For refined or white flours, all the husk and most of the germ are removed. There are also flours of varying degrees of coarseness with only a percentage of husk and germ removed. Stone-ground flour has been ground the old-fashioned way between millstones.

TYPES OF FLOUR

All-Purpose Flour, the standard home-baking ingredient, is white flour produced from a mixture of hard and soft wheats. It can be used for all types of breads and cakes, although it is a second choice for bread making behind bread flour. Both bleached and unbleached varieties are sold in supermarkets and health-food stores.

Barley Flour. To make a successful yeasted loaf this must be mixed with wheat flour because of its low gluten content. It can, however, be used for thin, flat breads and some unleavened breads.

Bread Flour, sold as white or whole-wheat, is milled from hard wheat, valued for its high gluten content. It also contains a small amount of malted barley and vitamin C, both of which contribute to making outstanding yeasted breads. If bread flour isn't stocked in your local supermarket, look for it in health-food stores.

Buckwheat Flour. Buckwheat is a seed, not a grain, so bread made from buckwheat flour alone is very crumbly and does not rise well. It should be mixed with wheat or rye flours to make bread, and is often used in Eastern Europe and North America to make pancakes, or blinis.

Chapati Flour is a finely ground wheat flour used in India to make many of the traditionl flat breads. It is sold in white and whole-wheat varieties from Indian grocers and some health-food stores.

Corn Flours Cornmeal is produced by grinding whole corn kernels. To make yeasted or sourdough breads, it is often mixed with wheat flour. For quick breads, it can be used along or with other grains or cereals.

In Mexico, tortillas are made from a fresh dough called *masa*. This is produced by first

𝒲hole-grain flours contain the husk, endosperm, and grain.

20

𝐹or centuries, water-mills and windmills have ground flour for the local community. Some, such as this one in St. Céré, France, are still working.

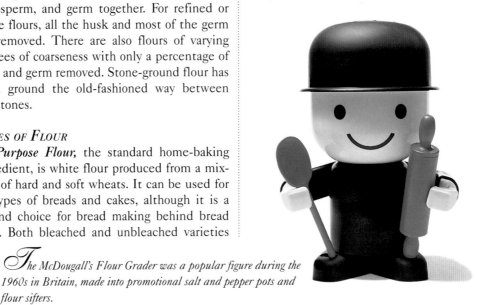

𝒯he McDougall's Flour Grader was a popular figure during the 1960s in Britain, made into promotional salt and pepper pots and flour sifters.

Flour of all types has been marketed under many different brand names. Some, such as Albatross, seem to bear no relation to the flour inside the packet.

simmering corn kernels in a solution of lime so they swell and the husks loosen. They are then pounded and ground to make them into a dough. For export, the *masa* is dried and broken up to produce *masa harina*, a coarse, yellow-brown flour.

Cracked Wheat is not really a flour, but broken wheat berries, available in coarse, medium, and fine textures. It can be soaked or simmered in water and added to a dough to produce a moist, dense texture (see Mixed-Grain Bread, page 48), or sprinkled dry over the tops of loaves before baking for a decorative effect.

Graham Flour was invented in the nineteenth century by a clergyman named Rev. Sylvester Graham. It is a coarse whole-wheat flour.

Gram Flour is made in India from ground chick-peas, or garbanzo beans, and is used to make chapatis and other flat breads.

Oat Flour and Oat Products. Oat flour is usually finely ground and makes a soft, moist loaf when mixed with wheat flour. Steel-cut oats, also called Scots oats, are fine or coarsely ground oat groats, popular with British bakers for adding moisture and an interesting texture to breads. Oatmeal, or rolled oats, can be used the same way.

Rye Flour is milled from a cereal grass, so it contains less gluten than wheat flours. This is why bread made with all rye flour is dense and not well risen. Dark rye flour contains the husk and germ of the grain as well as of the endosperm, while light rye flour contains mostly endosperm, with small amounts of germ and husk. Rye flours are slightly coarser than wheat flours. The sourdough method of baking bread (see page 22) is suitable for rye flour. Dark pumpernickel bread is an Eastern European specialty made with all dark rye flour.

Self-Rising Flour, particularly popular with southern bakers, is all-purpose flour (see above) with the addition of baking powder and salt; this makes it an ideal ingredient to use in quick breads. If a recipe calls for all-purpose flour, you can substitute self-rising flour, cup for cup, by omitting any salt and baking powder in the recipe. If you only have all-purpose flour when a recipe specifies self-rising, add 1½ teaspoons baking powder and ⅛ teaspoon salt to each cup of all-purpose flour.

Semolina Meal is made from a hard wheat called durum wheat, and consists of coarsely milled endosperm. It is more often used for making pasta than for making bread, and is not suitable for using in most cake or pastry recipes. Similar to farina, it is used in recipes like yellow cornmeal. Look for it in Italian grocery stores or health-food stores.

Whole-Wheat Flour is a result of milling the whole of the wheat berry to produce a coarse-textured, brown flour with higher levels of some nutrients and dietary fiber than white flour. It also has a higher fat content, so it should be stored in the refrigerator to prevent becoming rancid. The gluten content of whole-wheat bread flour varies with different brands across the country.

In this sixteenth-century woodcut, a farmer watches his sack of grain being poured into the hopper. This feeds the grain between the mill stones to be ground into flour.

Flour sifters, for the easy sprinkling of flour onto a worktop, are made in many shapes and sizes.

21

LEAVENING AGENTS

THE FIRST BREADS WERE SMALL, FLAT, AND UNLEAVENED. ONCE THE TECHNIQUE OF FERMENTATION WAS DISCOVERED, LEAVENED BREADS BECAME POPULAR AND WERE SOON UNIVERSALLY PREFERRED. THE FIRST LEAVEN BREAD WAS A KIND OF SOURDOUGH. THEN YEAST CAME INTO USE, AND IN MORE RECENT YEARS, CHEMICAL LEAVENING AGENTS HAVE BEEN ADDED TO BREAD-MAKING INGREDIENTS.

Baking powder was invented in the nineteenth century, and many brands with distinctive packaging and slogans have been produced over the years.

SOURDOUGH STARTERS

Breads made with what has come to be called a "sourdough" starter were the first leavened breads. Around 5000 B.C., probably by chance, someone left a rather liquid flour-and-water mixture in a warm place only to discover, maybe a day later, bubbles were forming on the surface and there was an interesting smell. As an experiment, more flour was added and the dough was baked, and the first risen loaf was produced, far superior in both flavor and texture to the hard, flat cakes that had been the staple diet of many people for thousands of years. It was soon realized, if a piece of this fermented dough was kept back, it could be mixed with a little more water and once again be put in a warm place, and the same process would take place. Bread mixtures ferment as a result of the natural yeasts that exist on the outside of every wheat grain, in the same way wine can be made using only the natural yeasts on the skin of the grapes.

Although yeast, a by-product of the brewing industry, was used during Roman times, most

Flour and Potato Starter

bread in Europe was made by the sourdough method until the seventeenth century. A small amount of starter dough could be kept at all times, and a good quality bread could always be baked, whether an individual was nomadic or settled.

When Europeans settled in New England, the sourdough technique went with them. Small amounts of starter were then carried west on

San Francisco Sourdough

San Francisco Sourdough

scant 1 cup bread flour
2 teaspoons sugar
1 cup warm water

Put the flour and sugar into a bowl. Stir in the water. Cover the bowl and leave it in a warm place, 2 days, or until it is bubbling and risen. This is enough to make up a loaf using 5 cups bread flour.

wagon trains, and along the Canadian borders and in the Pacific Northwest, lone trappers became known as "sourdoughs," because they were never without the means of producing a nutritious loaf.

Although yeast is now the main leavening agent used for bread, there are many countries in which sourdough loaves have remained firm favorites, notably Eastern Europe, France, and Germany, along with parts of the United States. Ciabatta, a new loaf from Italy, is made with a long rising time to give it a slight sourdough flavor.

Sourdough bread has a rich flavor and moist texture, and once the starter is made you will never have to worry about whether or not you have any yeast. A starter will take a few days to become active, but after the first batch it is a simple matter to keep several batches on hand.

Flour and Potato Starter

1 potato
3⅓ cups all-purpose flour, whole wheat-bread flour, or rye flour
1 cup plus 2 tablespoons sugar

Scrub the potato. Cut it in half. Boil and drain, reserving the water. Peel and mash it in a large bowl. Make up the potato water to 3½ cups with more warm water. Stir it into the mashed potato. Stir in the flour and sugar. Cover the bowl with plastic wrap and leave it in a warm place about 3 days, or until it is bubbling and smells sour.
Once it is at this stage, your starter will be alive. It can be used immediately or you can stir in another scant ½ cup flour and ⅔ cup warm water to keep it going.
To make a loaf using this starter, put three-quarters of the starter into a bowl and stir in enough flour to make a kneadable dough. Let the dough rise and bake it as normal.
Into the remaining quarter of starter, stir 2⅓ cups flour and 2 tablespoons sugar and 2½ warm water. Cover the bowl and return to its warm place.

YEAST

In the seventeenth century, a leaven made from brewer's yeast was made popular by the Flemish, and its use gradually spread. Still because there wasn't standard baker's yeast available, bread making was a hit-and-miss affair, regardless of the baker's skill.

In the nineteenth century, however, the French scientist Louis Pasteur discovered yeast is a living organism composed of a single cell. His research led to a reliable baker's yeast becoming commercially available. The species that is now used to make baker's yeast is *Saccharomyces cerevisiae*, which, when it is cultivated in warm, humid surroundings, reproduces itself rapidly.

Various types of yeast are available to the home baker today, and everyone has their own preferences.

Active-Dry Yeast is sold in ¼-ounce packages and 4-ounce jars. One package contains 2¼ teaspoons yeast, which is the equivalent of one 0.6-ounce cake compressed fresh yeast.

To use, put the amount of warm water (105° to 115°F) specified in your recipe into a bowl. Sprinkle the yeast on top, and leave in a warm place 15 minutes, or until the liquid begins to bubble. If you find a particular brand of yeast is slow to start fermenting, next time add 1 teaspoon sugar to the liquid before sprinkling the yeast on top; if you are using a brand of yeast you have not used before, experiment to determine how long it takes to ferment.

Compressed Fresh Yeast. Sold in supermarkets in 0.6-ounce cakes, this form of yeast is moist and crumbly. It is also very perishable, so it should be stored, unopened, in the refrigerator and used by the date indicated on the packaging. If you aren't going to use it immediately, however, it can be frozen. To use after it has been frozen, it should be defrosted at room temperature and used immediately.

Fresh yeast should be firm and moist, with a fresh scent, and should crumble easily between your fingers.

Recipes vary as to the amount of fresh yeast needed, but it is usually ½ to 1 ounce for 3 to 3½ cups flour.

To use fresh yeast, place a little warm water (105° to 115°F) in a small bowl (see individual recipes for specific amounts) and crumble the required amount of yeast into it. Leave 5 minutes in a warm place so the liquid begins to bubble. Then use as the recipe directs.

Quick-Rising Active-Dry Yeast, the most modern form of yeast, reduces the amount of time required for a bread dough to rise. It also has the advantage that it doesn't have to be reconstituted to use, like ordinary active-dry yeast, before it is combined with other ingredients. Instead, it is mixed with the flour and other dry ingredients before very warm (120° to 130°F) liquids are added. Sold in sealed ¼-ounce packages, this is interchangeable with compressed fresh yeast and active-dry yeast. Read the direction on the package and follow the recommended rising times.

CHEMICAL LEAVENING AGENTS

Chemical leavening agents are easy to use, and leavened loaves and cakes can be mixed and in the oven in minutes. This is because, although chemical raising agents begin to take effect in the dough or batter when liquid is added, they become more active in the oven. The main drawback of bread made with chemical leavening agents is that it is not as moist as yeasted or sourdough bread. It is best eaten almost as soon as it comes out of the oven, and certainly on the day it is baked.

Baking Soda is an alkaline leavening agent. Like yeast, it releases carbon dioxide when combined with an acid.

In most quick-bread recipes, such as soda bread and biscuits, ingredient such as soured cream, buttermilk, or plain yogurt are used. To neutralize the alkaline taste other acids suitable include lemon juice, cream of tartar, and molasses.

Baking Powder is a mixture of baking soda and cream of tartar to which a small amount of starch, has been added to act as an anticaking agent.

Active-dry yeast is in individual packages, each containing ¼ ounce, or 2¼ teaspoons, yeast

Baking powder and baking soda are fine, white powders. In quick-bread recipes they are mixed with the flour before any liquid is added.

OTHER BREAD INGREDIENTS

*THE ESSENTIAL INGREDIENTS OF BREAD ARE FLOUR, A LEAVENING AGENT, AND A LIQUID. BUT THERE IS NO
NEED TO STOP THERE. MANY OTHER INGREDIENTS ARE OFTEN ADDED TO ALTER THE FLAVOR AND TEXTURE
OF BREAD, RESULTING IN THE VAST RANGE OF DIFFERENT BREADS FROM AROUND THE WORLD.*

SALT

Salt is not just an extra ingredient. It is essential in most
bread recipes, even sweet ones. Bread baked without salt has
a strange, bland, sweetish flavor. Even a small amount of salt
will counteract this. On average, for a plain loaf, 2 teaspoons
salt are added for every 3 to 3½ cups flour.

Fine salt can be added to the flour before the yeast-and-
water mixture is stirred in. Kosher salt should be dissolved in
a little of the water before it is added so it is evenly
distributed. Do not, however, dissolve it in the same water
that you are using to start off the yeast. Salt will inhibit the
action of the yeast, because they should not come into
contact until the yeast has at least begun to ferment. In
recipes where a "sponge" is made with the yeast and some of
the given amount of flour to act as a starter for the dough, the
salt should be added to the second batch of flour.

LIQUIDS

Water is the main liquid used for most types of bread dough.
However, some or all of it can be replaced with another
liquid. All liquids should be heated to warm (see
temperatures under the specific types of yeast on page 23)
before they are added.

Milk is the most popular substitute for water. A milk loaf will
have a soft crumb and a thinner crust than bread made with
water. It may, however, become dry and stale more
quickly than an ordinary loaf. When milk is the
main liquid in soda bread, it should have a little
cream of tartar added to counteract the alkalinity
of the soda.

Fermented Milk Products, such as plain yogurt, cultured
buttermilk, or ordinary sour cream, produce a rich flavor and
a soft texture in a yeasted loaf. For quick breads made with
baking soda as a leavening agent, one of these ingredients is
essential to counteract the alkalinity of the soda.

Cream and Sour Cream Cream gives a rich texture to
yeasted loaves. When making scones, biscuits, or soda bread,
use sour cream for the same effect.

Vegetable Juices When you are making a loaf to go with
savory foods, such as soups and salads, a tomato or mixed
vegetable juice used instead of water adds a delicious, savory
flavor and an orange color. Carrot juice can be too sweet for
savory breads, but it can be used when making tea breads,
such as the Carrot Tea Bread (see page 109).

Fruit Juices can also be added to enrich sweet breads,
particularly those containing dried fruits. They are suitable
in both yeasted breads and quick breads. In yeasted breads
fruit juices give a mild, sweet flavor and a subtle color. Pure
orange juice is the most suitable.

Beer can be used to make strongly flavored breads with
whole-grain flours. It gives a distinctive, slightly bitter flavor.
Beer can also be used instead of water to make a sourdough
starter.

Eggs enrich and soften all yeasted breads and are best used
in combination with other enriching ingredients, such as
milk, butter, or oil. If used to replace all or part of the liquid
in a recipe, they can produce a loaf
which becomes dry after

24 hours. When you are replacing a liquid in a recipe with eggs, take into account their liquid measurement. The best way to ascertain this is to beat them in a measuring jug.

FATS AND OILS

Butter gives a moist, flaky texture to dough, and, if used in large quantities, a golden color. Unless otherwise stated, salted butter is used in the recipes in this book.

Margarine enriches a bread dough but does not give as good a flavor as butter. Use it only when small amounts are required, either in yeasted bread or in quick breads.

Butter Substitutes and Spreads These are not suitable for bread-making.

Olive Oil enriches, softens, and flavors many of the breads of the world, particularly those from Spain, Italy, and France. Often it is added with other liquid, in which case the amount of liquid you use may have to be reduced slightly. Other recipes call for the olive oil to be kneaded into the dough. This may sometimes appear to be an impossible task, but if the oil is added 1 or 2 tablespoons at a time and care is taken to knead it all in before adding the next spoonful, you will find it will all be incorporated.

Sesame Oil gives a rich, nutty flavor to a loaf. It can replace olive oil, but should be used only in small quantities in appropriate recipes, such as Middle Eastern breads.

Sunflower Oil enriches a bread dough in a similar way to olive oil, but does not give a very good flavor. It can, however, be used as a butter substitute in certain quick breads.

Vegetable Shortening is a soft, white fat. It is rarely used in yeasted breads but is sometimes called for in muffins and other quick bread recipes.

SWEETENERS

Sweeteners can be added to bread doughs in varying amounts. They may make the loaf very dark on the outside. This does not mean the bread is burned.

Brown Sugar adds color and a small amount of flavor to a loaf. It is often used in combination with a whole-wheat flour, when the crusts will not be white.

Granulated Sugar is used in a wide range of bread recipes, and is essential if you want to produce a white-colored crumb. It can be added to the flour with the salt or dissolved in the liquid before it is added.

Honey can be used for quick breads and muffins, as well as some yeasted loaves. It makes a sticky yeasted dough, so is rarely used for yeast breads in large quantities.

Molasses Small amounts of molasses make interesting yeast breads and quick breads (see Steamed Brown Bread, page 106).

Superfine Sugar is not necessary for most bread recipes, but may be specified in some quick-bread recipes because the fine grains dissolve quicker than those of granulated sugar.

FLAVORINGS

For even more variety, different flavorings can be added to doughs, and in most cases only small amounts are needed. Both fresh and dried herbs can be added to savory loaves. Spices added in fairly small quantities give flavor to both sweet and savory loaves. Ripe olives, sun-dried tomatoes, tomato paste, and garlic paste all add extra flavor to dough. Mashed potato makes a soft, moist bread. Dried fruits, candied cherries, candied peel, and chopped nuts are popular additions to enriched yeast breads doughs.

25

EQUIPMENT

MOST OF THE EQUIPMENT REQUIRED FOR SUCCESSFUL BREAD-MAKING IS ALREADY IN YOUR KITCHEN. IF YOU REGULARLY MAKE BREAD, YOU MAY WANT TO USE ONE OR MORE SPECIALIST ITEMS TO MAKE YOUR WORK EASIER AND IMPROVE THE APPEARANCE OF YOUR LOAVES.

BAKING TRAYS AND COOKIE SHEETS

Both nonstick and uncoated surfaces are available. Follow the manufacturer's directions before use. Although some recipes call for baking trays or cookie sheets to be greased, this makes them very difficult to clean and is rarely necessary. A dusting of flour will make life much easier. If it is essential to put bread on an oiled surface, cover your trays with aluminum foil and oil the foil. The foil can then be thrown away after use and your tray will be clean.

BOWLS

Large mixing bowls are essential for making bread. They should be big enough to allow you to knead the dough in the bowl, if the dough is very soft, and to leave the kneaded dough to rise without overflowing the bowl. Large bowls are also essential for mixing quick bread batters.

Small mixing bowls are useful for starting yeast, beating eggs, and combining small amounts of flavoring ingredients.

If you have a microwave oven, use microwavesafe bowls so you can warm and melt ingredients.

BREAD PANS

Standard loaf-shaped bread pans range in size from $3\frac{1}{2}$ x $1\frac{5}{8}$ x $1\frac{1}{2}$ inches to 10 x $3\frac{1}{2}$ x 3 inches, but the most common sizes for home use are 9 x 5 x $2\frac{1}{2}$ inches and $8\frac{1}{2}$ x $4\frac{1}{2}$ x $2\frac{1}{2}$ inches. The pans must be large enough to let the dough double in volume while it is rising before being put in the oven for baking.

Specialist bread recipes will call for other types of pans. Flat breads can be baked in shallow rectangular or square pans. Some loaves are made in round pans. Brioche molds are fluted and come in a variety of sizes for making loaves ranging from bun-sized to ones weighing more than 1 pound. *Kugelhupf* molds are also fluted but larger and ring-shaped.

All these pans are sold with standard or nonstick surfaces. All should be oiled lightly with sunflower or other oil before the first use. After this, nonstick pans may not need oiling, but follow the manufacturer's directions. You will also find bread pans made from metal and ovenproof glass.

BREAD-MAKING MACHINES

A bread-making machine takes all the work out of making bread. You put in the ingredients, set the controls, walk away, and a perfect loaf is ready at the time of your choosing. It is an excellent way to make fresh bread to order without having to put in any effort. Most bread machines come with a variety of cycles designed to handle specialty breads or to prepare the dough for hand-shaped breads and rolls. (See page 46.)

BRUSHES

Small, soft pastry brushes are used for oiling bread pans and also for brushing the surface of loaves with a glaze, such as beaten egg or oil, before baking. Buy the finest brushes you find so the bristles do not deflate risen doughs.

CLOTHS

Use clean dish towels to cover bowls of rising dough. Keep them separate from other kitchen cloths, wash after every use, and use them only for bread-making.

DOUGH SCRAPER

Although not essential, this is useful if you bake bread often. It is a plastic, rectangular, pliable scraper used for scraping dough from bowls and off work surfaces. It is sold in specialist bakeware stores and from mail-order suppliers

ELECTRIC MIXERS

An electric mixer with a dough hook successfully mixes bread dough. However, the baker's skill lies in being able to judge the correct consistency of the dough by its feel. It is also very therapeutic to make bread by hand. Whether you use an electric mixer or not is a matter of personal choice.

INSTANT-READ THERMOMETER

Available from kitchen-supply stores, one of these thin thermometers is ideal for checking the temperature of liquids.

MEASURING CUPS

Standard measuring cups are used for measuring flours and other dry ingredients in large quantities. For the recipes in this book, flour should be scooped out of the bag with an appropriate measuring cup. Scrape off the excess flour with a spatula before combining the flour with other ingredients.

MEASURING JUGS

Several measuring jugs of different sizes are useful. If you have a microwave oven, use microwavesafe jugs so you can warm or melt ingedients in them.

MEASURING SPOONS

Use for accurately measuring salt and small amounts of other ingredients, such as spices and herbs. Absolute accuracy is not essential with these ingredients but measuring spoons help you achieve consistently good results.

MICROWAVE

This is not essential but is an easy way of warming and melting ingredients.

ROLLING PIN

Some recipes require the dough to be rolled into a certain shape before baking, or rolled out thinly before being sprinkled with other ingredients, folded, and shaped. Use a long, straight, wooden rolling pin.

WORK SURFACE

A clear work surface is essential for making bread. If your kitchen countertops are smooth and clean, use them. If you have tiles or a rough-surfaced area, it is best to use a board or slab to knead your dough on. (Keep it specifically for that purpose.) A large marble slab is ideal. So, too, is a large plastic chopping board, as long as it has not been grooved by frequent cutting with sharp knives, or a large wooden board covered with a laminated layer. Always thoroughly clean and dry your work surface after use, so it is ready for next time.

Types of Bread

COMES IN ALL SHAPES AND SIZES, AND IN MANY DIFFERENT TEXTURES, COLORS, AND FLAVORS.
USING JUST ONE SIMPLE, BASIC MIXTURE, THE POSSIBILITIES ARE ENDLESS.

PLAIN BREADS

The basic loaf is made from flour, a leavening agent, salt, and water. It has a flavor that will complement sweet or savory dishes, and it can be sliced, cubed, or crumbled to form the backbone of many meals.

Yet, within that definition, bread can take many different forms. With only a slight variation of the mixing or baking method, or even a change of shape, the flavor and texture can be altered. The type of yeast or other leavening agent you use also makes a difference.

A basic plain bread dough can be made into loaves and rolls of many different shapes and sizes.

Plain loaves can be made from one type of flour or a mixture, allowing endless combinations and variations. They can be mixed with fresh yeast, active-dry yeast, or quick-rise active-dry yeast. Fresh yeast, in some cases, gives a more risen, lighter texture, whereas dried yeast often produces a close texture.

With plain breads, you can make small changes and additions to the ingredients without fundamentally changing their character: milk can be used instead of water; butter can be rubbed into the flour; or oil added with other liquids. A little added sugar produces sweeter breads, such as *Peineta* (see page 51) or *Massa Sovada* (see page 49)

A longer rising time than the usual one hour, such as is

needed to make Ciabatta (see page 53) or Fannie Farmer's Water Bread (see page 43), results in a richer flavor. The sourdough method produces yet an even richer flavor.

The final shape of a loaf also changes its texture. A flat bread, for example, has more of its surface exposed to the heat, so it has more crust. Some breads baked on a baking tray have a slightly drier texture than those baked in a pan. When dough is formed into rolls, there is even less crumb in relation to crust—this is why rolls do not stay fresh long.

Most breads are baked in a dry oven. Some recipes, however, require a pan of water to be placed in the bottom of the oven so the surface of the dough can be steamed, which softens the crust. A Baguette (see page 51) needs to be brushed with water to produce the classic crisp, crackling crust. Bagels (see page 52) are briefly immersed in boiling water before being baked, which makes the outside smooth and shiny. Other breads, such as English Muffins (see page 40), are baked on a griddle, giving them a moist texture and a thin, crisp outside.

ENRICHED BREADS

The main ingredients of enriched breads are similarly flour, a leavening agent, salt, and water, but larger proportions of other ingredients are added to change the flavor and texture.

Enriched breads can be made from a basic bread dough, with the addition of flavoring ingredients, such as dried fruits or olives (see page 25). A plain dough can also be used as a base for an open tart filled with a rich sweet or savory filling, or it can form the outside wrapping for a savory filling, as in Shrimp and Beansprout Buns (see page 70).

Enriching ingredients, such as butter, milk, and eggs, are often mixed into bread dough. The Sally Lunn (see page 62) and Brioche (see page 58) recipes are good examples of this. For some breads, enriching ingredients need to be added with a specific

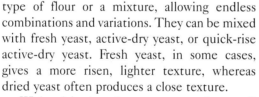

Bread dough can be enriched with butter, eggs, or milk, or other ingredients—such as chopped meats or nuts, or dried fruits—which can be kneaded in.

28

Thomas Muffett's Advice on Bread-Making

"Things to be observed in the well-making of Bread—whereof we must have great choice and care:

1. *of the Weate itself*   6. *of the Dough or Paste*
2. *of the Meal*   7. *of the Moulding*
3. *of the Water*   8. *of the Oven*
4. *of the Salt*   9. *of the Baking*
5. *of the Leaven*

All which circumstances I most willingly prosecute to the full, because as Bread is the best nourishment of all other, being well-made; so it is simply the worst being marred in the ill handling."

Thomas Muffett (1553–1604) *was a physician, a medical and scientific writer, and a poet, whose patients included members of the Court of Queen Elizabeth I. Fifty years after his death, his daughter, Patience, organized the publication of his book,* Health's Improvement, *which had been originally written in 1595.*

technique and sometimes both enriching ingredients and flavoring ingredients are added.

FLAT BREADS

Flat breads are variously made from yeasted, unleavened, and chemically leavened doughs. They can be baked in the oven or on the stove-top on a griddle, either plain or with a topping.

The first breads were made from unleavened dough, rolled into small rounds and baked on a hot stone, and this type of bread is still enjoyed today in many parts of the world. Indian Chapatis (see page 84) and Mexican Tortillas (see page 88) are thin and pliable and serve both as an eating utensil and an accompaniment to spicy foods. *Parathas* are slightly thicker and

eaten as an accompaniment. *Knackebrod* (see page 86) and Danish Crispbreads (see page 81), both from Scandinavia, are crisp and best eaten with cheese.

Yeasted flat breads should be baked until they are just cooked through, so even with their large surface area they are still soft enough to bend and to dip into other foods. They are popular in the Middle East, where many different types can be found at roadside markets and stalls. Pita Bread (see page 88) is baked at a very high temperature on heated trays so a pocket is formed. This is then usually stuffed with the filling.

The Italian pizza forms a base for a savory topping, and the same dough is folded around cheese or ham to make the rich snack known as Calzone (see pages 82-3).

Focaccia, slightly thicker but still soft in texture, can be made plain or can be topped with a variety of ingredients, from simple salt and chopped sage to a mixture of sliced vegetables.

British flat breads are often baked on a griddle, and the Germans and Austrians like to give flat breads a sweet topping and eat them with morning coffee or afternoon tea.

QUICK BREADS

The term "quick bread" refers to the fact the batter has been mixed quickly and does not require a long rising time. It does not necessarily mean the bread also bakes quickly.

Plain and flavored soda breads are usually quick to mix and quick to make. The same basic mixture can be cut into circles to make British scones, similar to biscuits, and it can be baked in the oven or on a griddle. *Roti* (see page 104) is a Caribbean, griddle-baked soda bread served with curries. Muffins (see page 99) are also a type of quick bread.

Sweet quick breads are a cross between bread and cake. They are generally too sweet and light-textured to be called "bread," but they are not as rich and light as a true cake. They are best served just warm or at room temperature sliced and sometimes buttered as a mid-afternoon snack, or as a simple dessert.

Flat bread can be baked in any size, but it is rarely more than ¹/₂ inch thick.

BASIC TECHNIQUES

THE BASIC TECHNIQUES OF BREAD-MAKING APPLY TO ALL TYPES OF BREAD. IT IS BEST TO BEGIN BY LEARNING HOW TO MAKE A PLAIN LOAF. ONCE YOU HAVE MASTERED THIS YOU CAN EASILY PROGRESS TO ADDING EXTRA INGREDIENTS OR MAKING A PARTICULAR SHAPE OF LOAF.

STEP-BY-STEP GUIDE TO MAKING A BASIC YEASTED LOAF

MAKES ONE LARGE LOAF

1²/₃ cakes compressed fresh yeast or 2 packages active-dry yeast

1¹/₄ cups warm water (105°–115°F)
3¹/₃ cups bread flour
2 teaspoons salt

Note: The quantity of water given here is the average quantity for the amount of flour. However, some types of flour, such as whole-wheat, can absorb more water, and so you may have to add a little extra if the mixture feels particularly dry. It is better to err on the wet side rather than the dry, since it is preferable to knead in more flour on the work surface than it is to add more water. The exact amount of water will also be affected by factors such as each brand of flour's absorbancy, the humidity, and the room's temperature.

The amount of flour given in a recipe is the amount needed to make a specific loaf. It does not take into account the small extra amount that you will need to flour your hands and the work surface before kneading the bread. Always have extra flour on hand for these purposes.

DISSOLVING THE YEAST

Put half the water into a small bowl. Crumble or sprinkle in all the yeast. Leave the yeast in a warm place, allowing 5 minutes for fresh yeast and 15 minutes for dry yeast. When the yeast starts to work, you will see small bubbles appearing in the liquid. The liquid does not have to be frothy; one or two small bubbles are all you need. On warm days, yeast will begin to work quickly. On very cold days, the process can take a little longer. You can speed it up by placing the bowl by a warm radiator or on the stovetop when the oven is turned on.

MIXING

Put the specified amount of flour into a large mixing bowl. If you are using fine salt, toss it into the flour with your fingertips. If you are using kosher salt, dissolve it in the remaining water. Make a well in the middle of the flour. Pour in all the yeast-and-water mixture

and, using a round-bladed knife, mix in a little flour from the edge of the well. Pour in the remaining water and begin to mix in the rest of the flour from the edge. Once the flour and water have been roughly mixed, begin using your hand to turn the flour until the water is incorporated and you have a lumpy, uneven dough. If the dough feels very stiff, add a little more water, 1 tablespoon at a time. If it feels very wet, work in a little more flour. These extra amounts will not inhibit the dough's rising, and if you take care at this stage, you will find kneading will be easier and the baked bread will have perfect texture with an even crumb.

KNEADING

Sprinkle flour over a clean work surface. Tip the dough out of the bowl onto the work surface, using your hands or a dough scraper to remove it all from the sides of the bowl. Rub off any dough sticking to your hands and then coat your hands with a little flour. Gather the dough into one lump. To knead the dough, first push it slightly away from you using the palms of both hands and then pull it back toward you with your fingertips. Continue to push and pull in this way, using a constant, rhythmic action. After about 10 times the dough will become elongated. Fold in both ends, give the dough a quarter turn, and repeat the process. After approximately 3 minutes the texture of the dough should become smoother.

Kneading also forces out any air pockets which can develop in the dough, causing it to rise unevenly. Continue kneading 5 to 7 minutes until it is smooth and elastic. Fold in the ends of the dough for the last time.

Place the dough on the work surface with the ends tucked underneath and rotate it to make it into a smooth, round ball. Return it to the bowl. Cut a cross in the top with a sharp knife, which will let the dough rise evenly. Unless otherwise specified, cover the bowl with a clean, dry dish towel.

KNEADING IN THE BOWL

Some recipes, such as Ciabatta (see page 53), require the dough to be much moister than for a standard loaf. Wet mixtures like this are always kneaded in the bowl. To do this, first flour your hands. Using your right hand, keep taking the sides of the dough to the middle as your left hand rotates the bowl in a clockwise direction. (If you are left-handed, knead with your left hand and rotate the bowl in an counter-clockwise direction with your right.) Even when the dough is wet, you will still be able to detect changes in texture. If the dough is dry enough, cut a cross in the top; if the dough is more like a thick batter, there is no need to do this. Cover the bowl with a clean, dry dish towel.

PROOFING

Put the bowl in a warm place away from drafts. The yeast will now begin the fermentation process that makes the dough rise. It needs to double in volume, and this usually takes an hour. However, in warm summer weather or in a hot kitchen the dough can be ready in 30 minutes. In a cold room, it can need much longer. You will also find that different types of dough rise at different rates. Often, the richer the loaf, the longer it takes to rise.

SECOND KNEADING

When the dough has risen sufficiently, return the bowl to the work surface. Punch down the dough with the back of your hand and then turn it onto the work surface. Knead it in the same way as before, pushing out any air pockets. This second kneading should take about 3 minutes. At this stage the dough should be very smooth, and you will need only a sprinkling of flour on the work surface and on your hands. The dough is now ready to be shaped and finished (see Bread

Shapes and Finishes, page 32).

SECOND PROOFING

Once the loaf has been shaped, it will need to stand in a warm place to rise for a second, shorter time. This should take only 15 to 20 minutes to rise. Some doughs will double in volume during this time; others, particularly the richer doughs, will rise only a little to rise considerably more during baking.

BAKING

Whatever type of bread you are baking, the oven should be preheated, so it is at the correct temperature when the dough is ready to be baked. Most breads are baked at 400°F, but follow the instructions given in the recipe.

Before moving your loaves from where they are proofing to the oven, make sure your oven racks are in the correct position and there is sufficient room above each loaf for it to rise freely. Transfer the loaves quickly and smoothly to their place in the oven.

A large loaf will take 35 to 40 minutes to bake in a standard oven. If you have a fan-assisted oven, however, it will take only 30 minutes, so check after this time to see if the loaf is done.

A completely baked loaf will be golden brown on the outside and will sound hollow when tapped on the bottom. If it doesn't sound hollow, return the unmolded loaf to the oven for 3 minutes and test again.

COOLING

Have a cooling rack ready. Take the loaf out of the oven and immediately turn it out of the pan or baking container, or lift it from the baking tray. Loaves that stay in hot pans can continue to bake for a little longer than is needed, and as they cool, they sweat inside the pan, producing a damp crust. Loaves baked on a baking tray will develop a thick, damp undercrust if they are left to cool on the tray.

Place the loaf on the cooling rack and leave until it is cool before serving. Bread eaten straight from the oven is still moist and steamy inside and has a doughy texture, and once the crust has been removed, the cut side will dry out.

BREAD SHAPES AND FINISHES

BREAD DOUGH CAN BE FORMED INTO MANY DIFFERENT SHAPES. IT SHOULD NEVER BE STRETCHED, BUT SHOULD BE EASED INTO SHAPE GRADUALLY SO IT WILL NOT SPRING OUT OF SHAPE DURING BAKING.

BAKING CONTAINERS

Standard Bread Pan The amount of dough made in the recipe given for the Basic Loaf will fit into a 9- x 5- x 2½-inch bread pan. Grease the pan lightly before you start to shape the loaf. After the last kneading, fold the sides of the dough into the middle and then, with your left hand on top of your right hand, press the dough out flat to a thickness of about 1½ inches so it forms a rectangle about the same length as the pan. Roll it up from one long side. Put the roll of dough into the pan with the end of the roll on the underside. Gently push the dough down several times with the back of your fist.

When dough has been sufficiently kneaded, it should feel smooth and not sticky. It is now ready to be shaped.

Round Containers Bread can be baked in round containers of various sizes. You can use a deep round cake pan or a French charlotte pan to make round loaves. A springform pan, 2 inches high, will make a loaf with an even-shaped base but a top that can rise both upward and sideways.

To shape a round loaf, fold the edges of the dough from the sides to the middle after the first kneading. Turn the dough over so the edges are tucked underneath. Then rotate the dough, tucking under the sides as you do so, to make a smooth round, dome shape.

Cylindrical Loaves Cylindrical hinged molds completely enclose the dough so it rises to fit the mold. Baking a loaf completely in one of these molds produces a thin crust and a very even crumb. These are sold at specialist bakeware stores.

Rectangular or Square Pans Some flat breads are baked in square or rectangular cake pans, usually about 2 inches deep.

Special Containers Breads such as French Brioche and Austrian *kugelhupf* are baked in special shaped molds, which can also be used for shaping plainer breads.

Ring Mold To make a ring of bread, shape the dough into a long, tapered rope. Coil it around the inside of a ring mold, over-lapping the tapered ends so the seam forms the same thickness as the rest of the loaf.

Flowerpot Loaves baked in a flowerpot were once popular. Use a new, terracotta flowerpot and leave it in a warm place for 24 hours to dry out. Grease it well with sunflower oil and put it into a preheated oven at 400°F for 45 minutes. Remove and leave to cool.

When completely cool, it can be used in the same way as a standard, metal bread pan. Never wash a flowerpot once it has been seasoned. Wipe it with paper towels after use.

La Cloche Bakers These are unglazed stoneware containers that produce a light loaf with a crispy crust. They are sold in specialist bakeware stores and from mail-order suppliers.

32

SHAPING LOAVES FOR A BAKING TRAY

Round Loaves A round loaf to be baked on a tray is shaped in the same way as for a round pan.

Cottage Loaf Divide the dough into 2 pieces of about one-third and two-thirds. Form each into a round shape and flatten both slightly. Place the smaller one on top of the larger one and press down evenly. Using the floured handle of a wooden spoon, make a hole down through the center of both pieces of dough. This gives the loaf shape and also makes sure both pieces of dough stick together.

Square Cottage Divide the dough into 2 pieces as for a cottage loaf, above. Form each piece into a square shape and place the smaller one on top of the larger. Using the floured side of your flat hand, make a slit-shaped hole right through both pieces of dough from top to bottom.

Spiral Make a long rope of dough. Coil it around from the center outward to form a spiral.

Cylinder Form a flat ball of dough and leave it on the work surface to rest for a few minutes. Flatten the dough with your hands to a thickness of about 1 inch. Roll up the dough and then roll it backward and forward under your hands, working from the center outward, to make a long, even rope. Flatten the dough out again into a rectangle. Fold both ends to the center and press down hard. This guarantees an even shape. Roll up the dough tightly from one long side to make an evenly shaped cylinder.

Ring Make a round loaf. Push the floured handle of a wooden spoon down through the center. Put 2 fingers into the hole made by the spoon and gradually work them around. With your fingers inside the hole and the palms of

To make a ring shape, first push the floured handle of a wooden spoon through the dough, then enlarge the hole with your fingers.

your hands on the edge of the ring, gradually ease out the dough to make the hole about 6 inches in diameter. Do this slowly and let the dough rest several times during the process.

BREAD SHAPES MADE BY SLASHING DOUGH

Slashing the surface of the dough with a sharp knife will make the loaf shape more interesting, as well as creating more surface area and therefore more crust. Various patterns can be made using long slashes down the center, short diagonal slashes across the length of a loaf, or even a checkerboard pattern on the surface of a large, round loaf. Some loaves take their shape and name from the type of slash commonly used when making them. Most slashes are made after the dough has risen for the final time, just before it goes in the oven.

Crown Shape the dough into a round and stand it on a baking tray. Score a circle in the top about 1 inch in from the edges. The center part will then rise above the rest.

MAKING A BRAID

Divide the dough into 3 equal pieces. Roll each piece underneath your hands, working from the center outward, to make a long, thin rope. Begin the braid from the center outward for an even shape.

Braid half the dough, and, as you near the end, stretch the tips and push them downward to shape and seal the ends. Form the other half of the braid in the same way.

As the loaf bakes, the braid should expand evenly to form a shape resembling an ear of wheat, as shown above.

The Coburg loaf is formed by making a flat round and then cutting a cross in the top. The corners of the dough formed by the cross will rise slightly higher than the rest of the loaf during baking.

Coburg This is a round loaf shaped by cutting a cross in the top. Make one long cut along the center, scoring the top of the loaf in half. Make the second cut in 2 halves, working from the center outward.

Checkerboard Make a round loaf. Score 3 parallel lines across the top. Score 3 more lines at right angles. Use smooth strokes.

Miche Form a round loaf and score the top into 6 sections. First make one long slash along the center of the loaf, not quite to the edges. Make the other slashes from the center of the first slash outward, again not quite to the edges of the loaf.

Bloomer Make a cylindrical loaf with tapered ends. Make diagonal slashes across the top about 1½ inches apart.

Vienna Loaf Make a cylinder shape with tapered ends. Cut one long slash lengthwise along the center.

Long Crusty Loaf Make a cylinder shape. Using a sharp pair of kitchen scissors, make diagonal cuts about 1½ inches long and downward into the dough to a depth of about 1 inch, forming a zigzag pattern along the center of the loaf. The cuts will spread apart as the loaf bakes.

Pain Brie Form a cylinder and taper each end. Make 4 parallel slashes along the length of the loaf.

Polka Make an elongated cylinder and score the surface to make a diagonal checkerboard pattern.

Baguette Roll the loaf into a long cylinder. Make 4 or 5 diagonal slashes along the loaf, staggering them slightly.

BREAD ROLLS

You can divide the basic bread dough into small pieces to make all kinds of interestingly shaped rolls. As a general rule, bread dough made with 3⅓ cups flour makes 16 rolls.

Round Rolls Divide the dough into small pieces. Place a piece of dough in the palm of one hand and roll the other hand, held flat, in a circular motion over the top. Round rolls can be left plain or can be slashed with one straight cut through the center, a cross, or several short, parallel lines.

Rings Make a round roll. Push your floured finger through the center and gently enlarge the hole to cover about one-third of the area.

Long Rolls Form the dough into a ball and then roll the ball between your hands to make a cylinder. Taper the ends.

Cloverleaf In a muffin pan, put 3 round balls together in each hole in a cloverleaf shape.

To make cloverleaf rolls, put 3 small balls of dough close together in each hole of a muffin pan tray. They join together as they bake.

34

Circle On a cookie sheet, arrange 8 rolls in a circle touching each other. They will stick together when baked.

Knots Roll the dough into a long, thin rope and tie it in a loose knot, taking care not to stretch it.

Parker House Rolls Roll out
the dough to a thickness of about ½ inch. Cut it into 3½-inch circles with a biscuit cutter. Brush them with melted butter. Score a line through the center of each circle with a sharp knife and fold the circle in half along the score, so the buttered sides touch. Put the rolls on a baking tray and gently press them down slightly.

BREAD FINISHES

Bread dough can be baked plain, or it can be given attractive finishes and glazes. Most loaves are coated or glazed immediately after shaping.

Flour Coating Dust the loaf with extra flour after shaping for an attractive, "country-style" appearance.

Egg Glaze After shaping, lightly brush the loaf with beaten egg.

Egg and Milk Glaze Beat together 1 egg and 2 tablespoons milk. This gives a less shiny surface than egg alone.

Milk and Sugar Glaze Use this for sweet buns. Warm ⅔ cup milk and dissolve 1 tablespoon sugar in it.

BREAD TOPPINGS

A topping should be sprinkled onto a loaf after glazing but before any slashing. It will add to the appearance of the loaf and also give added flavor to the crust. The most frequently used toppings are cracked wheat (usually on whole-wheat bread), poppy seeds, sesame seeds, caraway seeds, and cumin seeds. Slivered almonds and chopped nuts can be scattered over the top of sweet breads.

35

Different toppings—such as cracked wheat, chopped nuts, caraway seeds, sesame seeds, cumin seeds, slivered almonds, and poppy seeds—can change the appearance of many breads and rolls, as well as adding flavor and texture.

CHAPTER ONE

PLAIN BREAD AND ROLLS

ave fun exploring different cultures by experimenting with simple, basic mixtures of flour, yeast, and liquid to produce an astonishing variety of plain breads and rolls. Size and shape, along with kneading, proofing, and baking methods, all have their effect on the texture, flavor, and color of the baked loaf.

PLAIN BREAD AND ROLLS

Plain bread has long been the staple food in most parts of the world. The peasant bread of Spain, baked in large loaves, has been unchanged for several centuries. In contrast, the Italian ciabatta bread, shaped like a slipper and with a ripe, yeasty flavor, is one of the newest breads to be devised. In between, there is the crispy baguette, now almost synonymous with France, and the traditional American breads, Salt Risin' Bread, made from cornmeal and baking soda, on lonely farmsteads, where yeast was unavailable, and Fannie Farmer's Water Bread, light and white but long-keeping and created in her cooking school in Boston.

A plain bread dough can also be shaped into small rolls. Bread baked in individual portions include the light, soft rolls, made with small amounts of egg or milk; rolls for which the dough can be kept in the refrigerator until you need it; dense, delicious bagels, which are first boiled then baked; and traditional English muffins, cooked on a griddle.

Die Rast der Schnitter, *Pieter Brueghel (1564-1638)*

ENGLISH MUFFINS

English muffins are made with a moist yeast dough and baked on a griddle (a heavy iron plate). To serve, make a slit in each side of the muffin without splitting them apart. Toast them on each side under a hot broiler. After toasting, pull them in half and butter the soft, inner side. Muffins should be eaten on the day they are made.

MAKES 12 MUFFINS

¾ cup plus 2 tablespoons warm water (105° to 115°F)
2 cakes (0.6 oz.) compressed fresh yeast or 2 packages active-dry yeast
1 teaspoon sugar
6⅔ cups white bread flour or half white and half whole-
wheat bread flours
1 tablespoon salt
¾ cup plus 2 tablespoons warm milk (105° to 115°F)
2 tablespoons butter, softened
rice flour for dusting
oil or butter for greasing griddle

Put the water into a small bowl. Crumble or sprinkle in the yeast and add sugar. Leave fresh yeast 5 minutes and dry yeast 15 minutes.

Put the flour into a bowl and stir in the salt. Make a well in the center. Pour in the yeast liquid and milk. Add the butter. Using a wooden spoon, beat the ingredients together thoroughly. Knead by hand in the bowl until the dough feels smooth and elastic. Cover the bowl with a clean dish towel and leave it in a warm place for 1 hour, or until it has doubled in volume.

Knead the dough again in the bowl. Divide it into 12 portions. Coat a work surface with rice flour. Turn each portion separately in the flour to coat, then shape it into either a round or a square shape. Leave the muffins on the work surface, cover them with a dish towel, and leave to rise 20 minutes.

Brush a cast-iron griddle with oil or melted butter. Warm the griddle over low heat. Place as many muffins as will fit without touching on the griddle. (Use a pancake turner to transfer them.) Cook the muffins slowly, 8 to 10 minutes on each side; they should be a biscuit color and sound hollow when tapped. Regrease the griddle lightly between each batch, if necessary.

When the muffins are done, wrap them in a thick cloth until they are cool.

Pot Bread

Pot bread was created in South Africa in the nineteenth century by the Dutch Voortrekkers *traveling across the country in open wagons. They carried supplies of flour, but did not have any ovens. One of their essential pieces of equipment, however, was a heavy, cast- iron cooking pot with a lid and three legs, similar to the Dutch oven used by American pioneers. Sourdough leaven was used to make a dough, and when it had risen it was placed in the pot and covered with the lid. The problem of where to bake the loaf was solved by excavating an anthill, heating the inside with a wood fire, and placing the covered pot in it. Later, the three-legged pot was replaced by one with a flat base and straight sides, which could be placed in the ashes of a campfire.*

Pot bread is still popular. To make it, use an ordinary, plain bread dough (page 30), place it in an oiled, cast-iron casserole, and cover with the lid. In South Africa, a casserole containing pot bread is often baked in a fire pit and served at a braai,

A BOER FARM.

or barbecue. It can also be baked in an oven heated to 400°F for 40 minutes.

The loaf will bake into the shape of the pot and the top will be slightly cracked. Baking in a closed container produces a very yeasty flavor.

REFRIGERATOR ROLLS

These rolls are leavened by yeast, and the long fermenting process of the potatoes. The dough can be made in the conventional way and used immediately, or it can be kept for at least a week in the refrigerator. It can also be frozen for up to one month. Keeping a store of this dough is a good way to have freshly made rolls every day, without having to wait for the dough to rise. Simply go to the refrigerator and take out the required amount of dough. Once baked, the rolls have a very light texture and are best eaten fresh.

MAKES 20 TO 24 ROLLS

6 ounces floury potatoes	*1 teaspoon salt*
⅔ cup plus 2 tablespoons warm water (105° to 115°F)	*½ cup warm milk*
	1 egg, beaten
2 cakes (0.6 oz) compressed fresh yeast or 2 packages active-dry yeast	*4 tablespoons butter, cut into small pieces and softened*
	OPTIONAL GLAZE
3¾ cups white bread flour	*1 egg beaten with 1 teaspoon*
2 teaspoons sugar	*salt*

Scrub the potatoes. Boil them in their skins until tender. Peel and mash the potatoes; leave to cool. Put the water into a small bowl. Crumble or sprinkle in the yeast. Leave fresh yeast 5 minutes and dry yeast 15 minutes.

Put the flour into a large mixing bowl and stir in the sugar and salt. Make a well in the center. Pour in the yeast liquid and milk. Add the egg and butter. Mix to a dough and leave 5 minutes. Stir in the potatoes. Turn out the dough onto a floured work surface. Knead it until it is smooth. Return the dough to the bowl.

You can now leave the dough to rise in a warm place, then shape into rolls, leave to rise again, and bake at once. If you do this, cover the bowl. Alternatively, refrigerate for at least 12 hours, covered with plastic wrap.

After 12 hours in the refrigerator, the dough should have risen to the top of the bowl. If you are not going to use it immediately, punch it down, turn it over, and cut a cross in the top. Cover the bowl again, return it to the refrigerator, and use the dough when needed; it will keep for up to one week.

To bake the refrigerated dough, knead it on a floured work surface. Return it to the bowl, cover it with a clean dish towel, and leave it in a warm place 1 to 1½ hours, or until it has doubled in volume. Knead the dough again and form it into rolls (20 to 24 if using the whole amount at one time). Place them on floured cookie sheets, brush with the glaze, if using, and leave in a warm place 15 minutes. Meanwhile, heat the oven to 425°F.

Bake the rolls 15 minutes, or until they are golden brown and sound hollow when tapped on the bottom. Transfer to wire racks to cool.

FANNIE FARMER'S WATER BREAD

This is the first loaf in the "Bread and Bread-Making" chapter of *The Original Boston Cooking School Cookbook* by Fannie Merritt Farmer. Its characteristics are the use of boiling water to dissolve the butter, shortening, sugar, and salt, and the long rising time to produce a rich flavor, and which may well have been necessary in 1896 when the standard of yeast was variable. Fannie Farmer's original recipe used lard (beef fat) so the whiteness of the bread was not spoiled with too much butter. This modern version, however, uses vegetable shortening.

MAKES ONE LARGE LOAF PLUS 15 BISCUITS

1 tablespoon butter	*2 cakes (0.6 oz.) compressed*
1 tablespoon shortening	*fresh yeast or 2 packages*
1 tablespoon sugar	*active-dry yeast*
1½ teaspoons salt	*4 tablespoons warm water*
2¼ cups boiling water	*(105° to 115°F)*
	5 cups white bread flour

Put the butter, shortening, sugar, and salt into a large heat-proof bowl. Pour in the boiling water. Stir to dissolve the ingredients and leave until the liquid is lukewarm (105° to 115°F). Stir the yeast into the warm water and stir to dissolve. Leave fresh yeast 5 minutes and dry yeast 15 minutes. Add 4 cups of the flour. Knead the dough in the bowl until it is combined. Knead in the remaining flour.

Turn the dough onto a floured work surface and knead until it is smooth. Return it to the bowl and cover with a clean dish towel. Leave it to rise overnight at a temperature of about 63°F.

In the morning, make several slashes in the dough with a sharp knife and turn it over. Repeat the slashing and turning several times. Turn the dough onto a floured work surface and knead it again. Take off two-thirds of the dough, shape, and put in a greased 9- x 5- x 2½-inch bread pan. Roll out the remaining dough to a thickness of ½ inch. Using a 2-inch biscuit cutter, stamp out biscuits; this quantity will make about 15. Place the biscuits on a floured board. Leave the loaf until it has risen above the top of the pan and the biscuits until they are slightly puffy. Meanwhile, heat the oven to 400°F.

Bake the loaf 40 minutes and the biscuits 15 minutes, or until both are golden brown, risen, and the loaf sounds hollow when tapped on the bottom. Transfer to wire racks to cool.

PEASANT BREAD

This type of bread is typical of the everyday bread eaten throughout Spain. It is firm-textured and springy, with a crisp crust. Here it is made into a large tear shape, characteristic of the bread of the northern regions. Around Andalusia, in the south, however, loaves are often rectangular with slashed tops, and large, cushion-shaped loaves can be found all over the country. Frequently, peasant bread is stamped with the mark of the baker.

MAKES ONE LARGE LOAF

5 cups white bread flour	*2 cakes (0.6 oz.) compressed*
2¼ cups warm water (105° to	*fresh yeast or 2 packages*
115°F)	*active-dry yeast*
2 tablespoons milk	*1 tablespoon salt*

Put the flour into a bowl, reserving a scant ½ cup. Leave it in a warm place about 15 minutes. Put ⅔ cup of the warm water into a small bowl with the milk. Crumble or sprinkle in the yeast and leave in a warm place 5 minutes if fresh or 15 minutes if dry.

Make a well in the flour and pour in the yeast liquid. Do not stir, but sprinkle the remaining flour over the top. Cover the dough with a dish towel and leave in a warm place 1 hour, or until the yeast is frothy.

With your hand, knead the flour into the yeast from the edge of the well outward, until a fairly dry dough forms in the center. Sprinkle the salt around the flour that is still dry and then gradually add the remaining water to the well, drawing in the flour from the edge as you work. When all the water has been added and the dough is evenly mixed, turn it out onto a floured work surface and knead until it is smooth and soft. Return the dough to the bowl. Cover it with a dish towel and leave it in a warm place 1 hour, or until it has doubled in volume.

Knead the dough again and form it into a long oval shape, about 18 inches long and narrower at one end than the other. Place on a floured cookie sheet and flatten it slightly. Leave it in a warm place until it doubles in size. Meanwhile, heat the oven to 400°F.

Bake 45 minutes, or until the top is golden brown and the bottom sounds hollow when tapped. Transfer the loaf to a wire rack to cool.

43

SOFT ROLLS

Bread rolls can be made with a basic bread dough. However, if small amounts of extra ingredients, such as milk, eggs, or fat, are added the texture becomes much softer. The ingredients can be varied to suit availability and taste.

MAKES 16 ROLLS

⅔ cup plus 1 tablespoon warm water (105° to 115°F)

2 cakes (0.6 oz.) compressed fresh yeast or 2 packages active-dry yeast

3¼ cups white bread flour

2 teaspoons salt

3 tablespoons shortering or butter

¼ cup warm milk (105° to 115°F)

Put the water into a small bowl. Crumble or sprinkle in the yeast. Leave fresh yeast 5 minutes and dry 15 minutes.

Put the flour and salt into a large mixing bowl. Cut in the shortening. Make a well in the center and pour in the yeast liquid and the milk. Mix to a dough.

Turn the dough onto a floured work surface and knead until it is smooth. Return the dough to the bowl. Cover it with a clean dish towel and leave in a warm place 1 hour, or until it doubles in volume.

Knead the dough again and divide it into 16 equal pieces. Form each piece into a roll shape (for shapes, see pages 32–5). Put the rolls on a floured cookie sheet and leave in a warm place for 15 minutes to rise. Meanwhile, heat the oven to 400°F.

Bake the rolls 20 minutes, or until they are golden brown and sound hollow when tapped on the bottom. Instead of cooling them on a rack, keep them soft by wrapping them in a thick cloth so the steam is kept in as they cool.

Variations

Use a whole-wheat bread flour, or a mixture of half white and half whole-wheat, for a healthy alternative.

•

Replace ¼ cup of the liquid with 1 beaten egg; add it to the other ingredients with the milk for an even softer result.

•

Instead of milk, use ¼ cup plus 2 tablespoons warm water (105° to 115°F) and 2 beaten eggs; add the eggs when you would add the milk to make a rich and luxurious version.

The Sandwich

The combination of bread and meat or bread and cheese, with the emphasis on the bread, has been a standard meal for many centuries, probably almost since bread was first made. Putting the meat or cheese between two pieces of bread made the meal easy to carry and easy to handle and must have been practiced from an early time. French farmworkers in medieval times would eat a piece of meat between two slices of coarse bread, and similar meals were common in Mediterranean lands.

This people's meal went upscale in England in the eighteenth century, taking its name from John Montague, Earl of Sandwich. There are two theories given why this came about, but the truth is not known for certain. One story maintains the earl was an inveterate gambler who couldn't bear to leave the gaming table, even to eat. So his cook put meat, and probably pickles, between two slices of buttered bread. According to the other version, Montague was a keen sportsman who preferred to carry his lunch with him when hunting or shooting.

Whichever is correct, the new name gave what then became "the sandwich" a new lease of life, and sandwiches were often served at elaborate buffets provided by the English gentry in the eighteenth century.

Since then, sandwiches have become common all over the world. The English put them in lunchboxes, the French favor filling baguettes, the Scandinavians leave them open, and the Americans stack them high.

FINNISH RYE BREAD *with* CARAWAY SEEDS

The combination of white flour and whole rye flour in this recipe produces a light-textured but well-flavored loaf. It is a type of bread favored in Finland; caraway seeds are a popular flavoring throughout Scandinavia. The loaf is best eaten on the day it is made, and it goes well with preserves or cheese.

MAKES ONE LARGE LOAF

1¼ cups warm water (105° to 115°F)
2 cakes (0.6 oz.) compressed fresh yeast or 2 packages active-dry yeast
1 tablespoon dark brown sugar

1 tablespoon butter, softened
1⅔ cups white bread flour
1½ cups whole rye flour
1 tablespoon caraway seeds
1½ teaspoons salt

Put half the water into a large mixing bowl. Crumble or sprinkle in the yeast. Leave fresh yeast 5 minutes and dry 15 minutes. Stir in the remaining water, the sugar, and butter. Combine the two types of flour with the caraway seeds and salt. Make a well in the center and stir in the yeast liquid. Knead the mixture in the bowl until it begins to change texture. Cover the dough with a dish towel and leave in a warm place for 10 minutes. Turn it onto a floured work surface and knead it until it is smooth. Return the dough to the bowl. Cover it with the dish towel and leave it in a warm place for about 1 hour, until double in volume.

Knead the dough again and form it into a round loaf by tucking the edges underneath. Place it on a floured cookie sheet and leave in a warm place 20 minutes to rise. Meanwhile, heat the oven to 350°F.

Bake 40 minutes, or until the loaf has a hard, brown crust and sounds hollow when tapped on the bottom. Transfer to a wire rack to cool.

45

Bread-Making Machines

With a bread-making machine you can have fresh bread to order—with a minimum of effort and just a little planning.

Once learned, the basic bread-making process is easy, but for the days when you do not have time to knead, shape, and proof a loaf, bread-making machines do all the work for you. With one of these you can make anything from a plain white loaf to croissants and Chelsea buns.

Bread-making machines are a fairly recent invention, but they are becoming more and more popular as people realize, at a touch of a button, they can make bread when they choose. Kneading by hand is completely unnecessary, and because the process takes place in one container, there are not any dishes to wash.

Bread-making machines usually come with all the necessary equipment for measuring and mixing.

SETTINGS

Most machines have a choice of settings, letting you choose the type of bread you want to bake and how much time you are going to spend on it.

The most basic setting lets you put all the ingredients into the machine and then walk away until it is time to open the machine and take out a baked loaf. There is sometimes a faster version of this basic setting.

Some machines have a program for adding ingredients. A beeper will sound when it is time to add dried fruits, or other such ingredients, so they are not crushed by the kneading process.

The "dough" setting is used if you want the machine to mix and knead the dough for you, leaving you to take it out and shape it as you want. This is useful if you want to make rolls instead of bread or if a loaf has to be baked in a characteristic pan such as a *Kugelhupf* mold.

Some machines have separate programs for white and whole-wheat or multigrain flours. They may also have programs for adapting conventional recipes.

Tips for Using a Bread-Making Machine

- *Always refer to the manufacturer's directions before beginning a loaf. These will tell you the correct program to use.*
- *Keep the inside of the machine clean.*
- *Place the machine on a firm, dry worktop not covered with a tablecloth or any other textile. There should be a distance of at least 2 inches between the machine and the wall or any other object.*
- *Keep the machine out of reach of children.*
- *Do not use the machine near a heat source or in rooms where the humidity is high.*
- *Do not cover the machine when it is in use.*
- *Never remove the bread pan when the machine is in use; this upsets the program.*
- *Use oven mitts when taking the bread out, because both machine and bread will be very hot.*

TIMER

The basic bread-making program is 3 to 5 hours. You can, however, set the timer for up to 13 hours on most models. This is particularly useful if you are out all day and want to come home to fresh bread, or if you like to wakeup to freshly baked bread for breakfast.

INGREDIENTS

The same ingredients are used in a machine as for breads baked conventionally. You can choose the type of flour you use, provided you follow the methods and settings recommended by the manufacturer.

A quick-rise active-dry yeast is recommended. It is put directly into the bread pan and should never be mixed with water first. The manufacturer's directions, however, will specify the type of yeast most suitable for your model.

Use ordinary table salt only, not a kosher sea salt or a low-sodium substitute.

If you are using fat, butter gives the best flavor and texture.

Liquids are used cold, not warm, as all the heating necessary is done by the machine. Milk can be used instead of water, but only dried milk powder can be used with most overnight programs.

Eggs and other fresh ingredients, such as chopped onion, can be added at the appropriate times (see manufacturer's directions), but, like milk, should not be added to bread being baked on the timer setting because they might become stale during the long waiting period.

Basic White Loaf Recipe for a Bread-Making Machine

Makes one large loaf

1 teaspoon quick-rise active-dry yeast
3⅓ cups white bread flour
1 tablespoon sugar
2 tablespoons butter
2 tablespoons dried milk powder
1½ teaspoons table salt
1½ cups cold water

Take the bread pan out of the machine and mount the kneading blade on the shaft.
Put the yeast in the bottom of the bread pan. Add the flour, sugar, butter, milk powder, and salt.
Pour in the water.
Put the bread pan back into the machine, making sure it touches the bottom of the compartment.
Close the lid. Plug in the machine.
Select the menu you want: for example, Bake, Rapid Bake, or Timer. Press Start.
The machine will make a beep or other noise when the bread is ready. As soon as this happens, open the lid and take out the bread pan.
Turn the bread pan upside down and shake it several times to remove the loaf.
Place the loaf on a wire rack.
Unplug the machine and leave to cool.

Mixed-Grain Bread

This type of bread, made with cracked wheat and a mixture of whole-grain flours, is a favorite in New Zealand, where rich, high-fiber breads are a popular part of a healthy diets. Cracked wheat is available from health-food stores and supermarkets. The mix of ingredients and the single rising period produce a very loose-textured, moist, crumbly loaf, which sometimes has holes running through it. This is a characteristic, and not a mistake in your technique! The flavor is on the sweet side because so little salt is added.

MAKES ONE LARGE LOAF

1 cup cracked wheat
2½ cups cold water
1¼ cups warm water (105° to 115°F)
2 cakes (0.6 oz.) compressed fresh yeast or 2 packages

active-dry yeast
4 tablespoons skim milk powder
1¾ cups whole-wheat flour
2⅓ cups whole rye flour
1 teaspoon salt

Put the cracked wheat into a saucepan and cover it with the cold water. Bring it to a boil. Lower the heat and simmer 1 minute. Remove from the heat and drain; cool to lukewarm.

Put about one-third of the warm water into a large mixing bowl. Crumble or sprinkle in the yeast. Leave fresh yeast 5 minutes and dry 15 minutes. Stir in the remaining water, the skim milk powder, and the cracked wheat. Mix both types of flour together with the salt. Gradually mix the flours into the cracked-wheat mixture to make a moist dough. Knead the dough in the bowl until it begins to change texture and become elastic.

Put the dough into a greased 9- x 5- x 2½-inch bread pan. Leave in a warm place 30 minutes to 1 hour, or until the dough rises about ½ inch above the edge of the pan. Meanwhile, heat the oven to 400°F.

Bake the loaf 45 minutes, or until it sounds hollow when tapped on the bottom. Transfer to a wire rack to cool.

Massa Sovada

Massa Sovada is an interestingly shaped, sweet bread. It comes from Portugal and the dough is rolled around in a spiral shape, known as a *caracois*, or "snail." The bread is firm-textured and sweet, and good served with preserves or as an accompaniment to fruit compotes. Day-old bread is also very good toasted.

MAKES ONE LOAF

4 tablespoons warm water (105° to 115°F)	1 teaspoon salt
1 cake (0.6 oz.) compressed fresh yeast or 1 package active-dry yeast	7 tablespoons warm milk (105° to 115°F)
2½ cups white bread flour	1 egg, beaten
6 tablespoons sugar	3 tablespoons unsalted butter, cut into small pieces and softened

Put the water into a small bowl. Crumble or sprinkle in the yeast. Leave fresh yeast 5 minutes and dry 15 minutes.

Put two-thirds of the flour into a large mixing bowl and stir in the sugar and salt. Make a well in the center. Pour in the yeast liquid, the milk, and the beaten egg. Using your hand, gradually bring in flour from the edge of the well. Beat in the butter and then the remaining flour, a little at a time. Turn the dough onto a floured work surface and knead until it is smooth. Return the dough to the bowl. Cover it with a clean dish towel and leave it in a warm place 1 hour, or until it doubles in volume.

Knead the dough again and form it into a long rope about 1½ inches thick. Flour a 9-inch shallow cake pan. Starting from the center, spiral the rope of dough inside the pan. Heat the oven to 350°F. Leave the loaf in a warm place 15 minutes to rise.

Bake 40 minutes, or until the loaf is golden brown and sounds hollow when tapped. Transfer to a wire rack to cool.

Salt Risin' Bread

Salt Risin' Bread is a farmhouse bread, made with baking soda as the leavening agent but left for a long time to rise like a yeast dough. Made with a mixture of cornmeal and cake flour, it has a dense texture, with a soft crumb and a thin, golden crust. It goes well with most accompaniments from sweet preserves to a rich stew. The long rising time precludes Salt Risin' Bread from being the kind of loaf you would make daily, but it was originally made in the days when it was not unusual to make enough loaves in one batch to last one family for a week.

MAKES ONE LARGE LOAF

½ cup yellow cornmeal	3 cups plus 1 tablespoon cake flour
2 teaspoons sugar	½ teaspoon baking soda
2 teaspoons salt	2 tablespoons vegetable shortening
1 cup plus 2 tablespoons milk, boiling	

Put the cornmeal into a large heatproof mixing bowl with 1 teaspoon each of the sugar and salt. Stir in the boiling milk. Cover the bowl and leave it in a warm place 12 hours, by which time the batter should have started to form bubbles.

Stir in one-third of the flour, the remaining salt and sugar, and the baking soda. Cover the mixture again and leave it in a warm place to rise 3 hours; it may start to smell unpleasant at this stage, but this is just a product of the fermentation and will not give an unpleasant flavor to the loaf. After 3 hours, the dough should have risen.

Heat the oven to 350°F. In the bowl, knead in the remaining flour and the shortening. Form the mixture into a loaf shape and put it into a greased 9- x 5- x 2½-inch bread pan; an additional rising isn't necessary.

Bake 50 minutes, or until it is golden brown. Transfer to a wire rack to cool.

PEINETA

Plain, sweetened breads called *pan dulce* have been popular in Mexico since the first sugar cane was grown there in the fifteenth century. The special attraction about *peineta*, translated as "comb bread," is its interesting shape, similar to a cock's comb. It is soft, very slightly sweet, and with a thin crust. It is best eaten with preserves.

MAKES ONE LOAF

½ cup warm water (105° to 115°F)
1 cake (0.6 oz.) compressed fresh yeast or 1 package active-dry yeast
6 tablespoons warm milk (105° to 115°F)
2 tablespoons shortening
2 tablespoons sugar
1 egg, beaten
2¼ cups plus 2 tablespoons white bread flour
1 teaspoon salt

Put the water into a large mixing bowl. Crumble or sprinkle in the yeast. Leave fresh yeast 5 minutes and dry 15 minutes. Add the milk, shortening, sugar, and egg. Mix the flour with the salt, stir it into the liquids, and mix to a dough. Turn the dough onto a floured work surface and knead until it is smooth. Return the dough to the bowl. Cover it with a clean dish towel and leave it in a warm place 1 hour, or until it has doubled in volume.

Knead the dough again. Roll it out into a circle about 10 inches across and ¾ inch thick. Lift the dough onto a floured cookie sheet. Using sharp kitchen scissors or a sharp knife, make slits all around the outside edge, about ¾ inch long and ¾ inch apart. Fold the dough circle nearly in half so the upper layer is about 1 inch short of meeting exactly with the edge of the lower layer. Ease the corners backward, away from the edge, so the loaf becomes a crescent shape. Leave it in a warm place 20 minutes to rise. Heat the oven to 350°F.

Bake 30 minutes, or until the top is golden brown and the bottom sounds hollow when tapped. Transfer the loaf to a wire rack to cool.

Don Quixote

"With the bread eaten up, up breaks the company."

MIGUEL DE CERVANTES, 1547–1616

BAGUETTES

This is the classic, long French loaf, crisp on the outside and soft in the middle, always best eaten on the day it is made. For the most authentic effect, baguettes should be made with a large proportion of ordinary cake flour, rather than hard bread flour. In commercial bakeries, the crisp crust is achieved by jets of steam released inside the ovens. The steam causes the surface of the loaves to become initially very soft and then, when the steam is turned off, to become hard and crisp in the dry heat. A substitute for this method is to brush the loaves repeatedly with water as they bake.

MAKES 4 BAGUETTES, EACH APPROXIMATELY 14IN LONG

2 cups warm water (105° to 115°F)
2 cakes (0.6 oz.) compressed fresh yeast or 2 packages active-dry yeast
1½ teaspoons salt
4 cups plus 2 tablespoons cake flour
⅔ cup white bread flour

Pour ⅔ cup of the water into a small bowl. Crumble or sprinkle in the yeast. Leave fresh yeast 5 minutes and dry 15 minutes. Dissolve the salt in the remaining water.

Mix the two types of flour together in a large mixing bowl. Make a well in the center and pour in the yeast liquid. Mix in a little of the flour from the edge of the well. Gradually add the salted water, mixing in the remaining flour as you do so.

Turn the dough onto a floured work surface (use cake flour rather than bread flour) and knead it until it is smooth. Return the dough to the bowl. Cover it with a clean dish towel and leave in a warm place 1 hour, or until it doubles in volume.

Knead the dough again and divide it into 4 equal pieces. Roll each piece into a long, thin loaf about 14 inches long and place on a floured cookie sheet. Leave the loaves in a warm place to rise 30 minutes. Meanwhile, heat the oven to 400°F and place a baking pan of boiling water in the bottom of the oven.

Brush the loaves with cold water and, using a sharp knife, make regular diagonal slashes along the length for a traditional appearance.

Bake 1 hour, brushing the baguettes with cold water every 15 minutes. When done, they should be very crisp and golden. If they look like they are browning too quickly, cover them with crumpled aluminum foil.

Transfer the loaves to wire racks to cool. Eat on the day of baking.

BAGELS

Bagels originated in Austria, where they were called *Beugeln*, meaning "rings," referring to their shape. They are a favorite food in Jewish communities all around the world. Bagels are dropped into boiling water before baking, and this gives them a firm, but light, texture and a shiny surface. Bagels are traditionally served split, spread with cream cheese, and topped with a smoked fish such as salmon or herring.

MAKES 16 BAGELS

1 cup plus 2 tablespoons warm milk (105° to 115°F)
1 cake (0.6 oz.) compressed fresh yeast or 1 package active-dry yeast
4 tablespoons butter, cut into small pieces and softened
2 tablespoons sugar

1 egg, separated
½ teaspoon salt
2¼ cups plus 2 tablespoons white bread flour
oil for greasing
1 tablespoon poppy or sesame seeds or kosher salt for topping

Put the milk into a large mixing bowl. Crumble or sprinkle in the yeast. Leave fresh yeast 5 minutes and dry 15 minutes.

Stir in the butter, sugar, egg white, and salt. Gradually mix in the flour to make a soft dough. Turn the dough onto a floured work surface and knead until it is smooth. Return the dough to the bowl. Cover and leave in a warm place for 1 hour, or until it doubles in volume.

Knead the dough again and divide it into 16 equal-size pieces; form each piece into a flat circle. To make the bagel shape, flour your forefinger and push it down through the center of the dough. Gently work your finger around in a circle to enlarge the hole. Make the hole bigger by twirling the bagel around and around until it makes up about one-third of the diameter of the dough. When all the bagels are shaped, place them on a floured work surface, cover them with a dish towel, and leave to rise 10 minutes. Cover 3 cookie sheets with foil and lightly oil the foil. (Bagels are wet and will stick if this is not done.) Meanwhile, heat the oven to 400°F.

Bring a large pan of water to simmering point, so the water is just trembling; maintain it at this temperature. Drop the bagels into the water, a few at a time so they stay separate. Leave them in the water about 15 seconds, or until they begin to swell. Lift them out with a draining spoon and place on the prepared cookie sheets.

Brush the bagels with the egg yolk and scatter them with your chosen topping. Bake 20 minutes, or until they are golden brown and sound hollow when tapped on the bottom. Transfer to wire racks to cool. During baking, the hole in the center may close up and becomes simply an indentation.

OATMEAL *and* POTATO BREAD

This is based on a German recipe called *Kraftbrot mit Haferflocken. Kraftbrot* is usually bread made with white flour with added wheat germ, and one of its uses is for open sandwiches. In this recipe, the wheat germ has been replaced by oatmeal. The addition of potatoes makes the bread springy and close textured, and the crust is thin and golden. It makes very good open sandwiches.

MAKES ONE LARGE LOAF

5 ounces floury potatoes
1 tablespoon butter
1¼ cups warm water (105° to 115°F)
2 cakes (0.6 oz.) compressed

fresh yeast or 2 packages active-dry yeast
3⅓ cups white bread flour
2 cups oatmeal

Scrub the potatoes. Boil them in their skins until tender (this gives a better flavor and texture). Peel and mash the potatoes with the butter; leave to cool.

Put the water into a large mixing bowl. Crumble or sprinkle in the yeast. Leave fresh yeast 5 minutes and dry yeast 15 minutes. Stir in the flour to make a moist dough. Cover the dough with a dish towel and leave it in a warm place 1 hour, or until it doubles in volume.

Add the oatmeal and potatoes to the dough. Turn the dough onto a floured work surface and knead about 15 minutes, or until it is smooth and bubbles appear in the surface. Shape the dough and put it into a greased 9- x 5- x 2½-inch bread pan. Leave in a warm place 30 minutes to rise. Meanwhile, heat the oven to 350°F.

Bake 50 minutes, or until the top is golden brown and bottom sounds hollow when tapped. Transfer the loaf to a wire rack to cool.

CIABATTA

Ciabatta is a relatively new bread, developed in the area around Lake Como in Italy. Ciabatta means "slipper" and the bread is so called because of its slipperlike shape. The characteristic nutty, slightly sour flavor is produced by the two long rising periods. It rises well in the oven to make a beige-colored loaf with a thin, soft crust, a soft, holey crumb, and a springy texture.

MAKES TWO LOAVES

2½ cups warm water (105° to 115°F)	1 teaspoon sugar (for active-dry yeast only)
2 cakes (0.6 oz.) compressed fresh yeast or 2 packages active-dry yeast	5⅓ cups white bread flour
	6 tablespoons olive oil
	1 tablespoon salt

Put ⅔ cup of the water into a small bowl. Crumble or sprinkle in the yeast; add the sugar if using dried yeast. Leave fresh yeast 5 minutes or dry 15 minutes.

Put about two-thirds of the flour into a large mixing bowl. Gradually stir in the yeast liquid, the olive oil, and all the remaining water. Knead the mixture with your hand in the bowl, taking the side of the mixture to the middle with one hand and turning the bowl with the other. It will be a very moist, thick batter. Cover the dough with a clean dish towel and leave it in a warm place 4 hours, or until bubbly and it doubles in volume.

Add the salt to the rest of the flour. With your hand, knead the salted flour into the dough still in the bowl; it will be a very wet mixture. Cover the bowl with the dish towel again and leave it in a warm place 1 hour longer.

Heat the oven to 425°F. Coat 2 baking trays liberally with flour. Knead the dough in the bowl again and divide it into 2 portions with your hand; the dough will be moist but springy. Tip each piece out onto a prepared tray. If necessary, gently push the dough around the edges to make it slightly wider at one end than the other. Dust it with more flour. Leave the loaves in a warm place 10 minutes to rise.

Bake 30 minutes, or until the loaves are golden brown, risen, and sound hollow when tapped on the bottom. Transfer them to wire racks to cool.

CHAPTER TWO

ENRICHED BREADS

Treat yourself to the addition of savory or sweet fillings—or of milk, eggs, butter, oil, or sugar—to widen the scope of your bread-making. From the traditional to the newly created, enriched breads can be meals in themselves, substantial snacks, or wickedly sumptuous teatime or coffeetime treats.

ENRICHED BREADS

Roll a sumptuous olive-oil-bread dough around a savory or sweet filling and you have a loaf, originally from the Middle East, that is good to look at and flavorful and substantial to eat. Roll out a similar dough and fold it around spices, sugar, and dried fruits and you have Dough Cake, a rich, sweet treat from an English cottage. Bread dough can also make small, savory packages to be baked or steamed. When the added ingredients are kneaded into the dough, the whole texture of the loaf changes. The Sally Lunn, for example, is rich and golden and almost cakelike in its lightness; the brioche is firmer textured and makes wonderful toast; and a freshly made croissant is light and flaky.

Other breads—such as anchovy bread and Christmas fruit loaf—are both enriched and flavored, with extra ingredients being kneaded into the dough. And from Switzerland enjoy a cheese and onion tart with a rich bread "crust."

Afternoon Tea, *Kate Greenaway 1886*

57

BRIOCHE

The brioche is the favorite rich bread of France. It is best eaten fresh and slightly warm but, when a day old, it makes excellent toast. The classic brioche is made in a conical, fluted mold with a small portion of dough on top of the main loaf. Large and small molds are available. However, if you do not have the right molds, use ordinary round deep cake pans, small ring molds or 3-cup half round bowls, for the larger brioches, and ramekins for the smaller ones.

MAKES 2 LARGE · 12 SMALL BRIOCHES

4 tablespoons warm water (105° to 115°F)
1 cake (0.6 oz.) conpressed fresh yeast or 1 package active-dry yeast
2½ cups white bread flour
1 teaspoon salt

3 eggs, beaten
¾ cup (1½ sticks) butter, cut into small pieces and softened
GLAZE
1 egg yolk beaten with 1 teaspoon water

Put the water in a small bowl. Crumble or sprinkle in the yeast. Leave fresh yeast 5 minutes and dry 15 minutes.

Put the flour into a bowl and add the salt. Make a well in the center. Pour in the yeast liquid and stir a little of the flour into it. Stir in the beaten eggs and add the butter. Mix to a dough.

Turn the dough onto a floured work surface and knead it until it is smooth and all the butter has been incorporated. Return the dough to the bowl. Cover it with a clean dish towel and leave it in a warm place 1 hour, or until it doubles in volume.

Knead the dough again. Return it to the bowl, cover it, and chill at least 1 hour; this firms the butter and makes shaping the dough easier.

Grease 2 large or 12 small brioche molds. Knead the dough lightly once more. Divide the dough into the correct number of portions to suit your molds. For a classic brioche shape, divide each piece of dough into pieces of two-thirds and one-third. Form the larger piece into a ball and put it into the prepared mold. Make a hole in the center. Shape the smaller piece into a cylinder, wider at the top than the bottom. Insert the narrow end into the hole in the larger piece of dough so the end protrudes and looks like a ball of dough sitting on the top.

Leave the brioches in a warm place 30 minutes, or until the base has risen to the top of the mold. Meanwhile, heat the oven to 400°F. Brush the tops with the egg-and-water glaze. Bake large brioches 25 minutes and small ones 10 minutes; they should be golden brown and sound hollow when tapped on the bottom. Transfer to wire racks to cool.

The King's Breakfast

"The King asked
The Queen, and
the Queen asked
the Dairymaid:
'Could we have some butter for
The Royal slice of bread'?"

A. A. MILNE, 1882–1956

ROLLED BREAD

Roll a delicious and easy bread dough, enriched with olive oil, around a choice of simple fillings and you create a flavorful, delicious loaf. Those made with savory fillings are a tempting, easy snack or an exciting accompaniment to cheese, salads, casseroles, and soups. Rolled bread with a sweet filling can be served with coffee or tea, midmorning or midafternoon.

MAKES TWO 16-INCH LONG LOAVES

1¼ cups warm water (105° to 115°F)
1 cake (0.6 oz.) compressed fresh yeast or 1 package active-dry yeast

2 tablespoons olive oil
3⅓ cups white bread flour
½ teaspoon salt

Put the water into a large mixing bowl. Crumble or sprinkle in the yeast. Leave fresh yeast 5 minutes and dry 15 minutes.

Add the oil. Stir in the flour and salt, stirring to form the mixture into a dough. Turn it onto a floured work surface and knead until smooth and elastic. Return it to the bowl and cover with a clean dish towel. Leave in a warm place 1 hour, or until it doubles in volume.

Prepare your chosen filling (see below).

Knead the dough again and divide it into 2 equal pieces. Roll each piece into 16- x 8-inch rectangle. Spread the filling evenly over each piece of dough. Roll up each piece of dough from a long side. Place the rolled loaves, seam downward, on a floured cookie sheet. Pinch the ends to seal them and make a pointed shape. With a sharp knife, cut several slashes on each loaf.

Leave the loaves in a warm place 20 minutes to rise. Meanwhile, heat the oven to 375°F. Bake 30 minutes, or until both loaves are golden brown and sound hollow when tapped on the bottom. Transfer to wire racks to cool.

Fillings

(each is enough for 2 loaves)

Cheese and Onion Filling

2 onions, finely chopped
3 tablespoons olive oil
4 ounces feta cheese

Soften the onions in the olive oil over medium heat. Spread the onion slices evenly over the dough. Cut the cheese into very small, thin slivers and scatter them over the onions.

Herb and Garlic Filling

6 tablespoons chopped fresh chervil or parsley
2 tablespoons chopped fresh tarragon
2 tablespoons chopped fresh thyme
2 garlic cloves, chopped
4 tablespoons olive oil

Mix all the ingredients together. Spread evenly over the 2 pieces of dough.

Olive Filling

2 onions, finely chopped
3 tablespoons olive oil
20 ripe olives

Soften the onions in the oil over medium heat. Spread the slices evenly over the 2 pieces of dough. Pit and halve the olives. Scatter them evenly over the onions.

Walnut and Date Filling

¾ cup shelled walnuts
4 ounces dates, pitted
1 teaspoon ground cinnamon
4 tablespoons butter, melted

Very finely chop or grind the walnuts. Finely chop the dates. Put them into a bowl and stir in the cinnamon and melted butter. Spread the filling evenly over the dough.

CROISSANTS

The croissant was devised in Austria but has come to be associated with France. The yeast dough for croissants is easy to make, but combining it with butter, which has to be chilled to produce the flaky, layered texture, makes the process time-consuming. In France, croissant bakers put their dough into special cabinets, which change temperature at regular intervals. To make croissants at home, however, the dough must be taken in and out of the refrigerator. The end result, however, is worth it, when golden croissants come out of the oven, crispy and flaky on the outside and soft in the middle.

MAKES ABOUT 12 CROISSANTS

1 cup plus 2 tablespoons warm water (105° to 115°F)	*2 tablespoons sugar*
	1 teaspoon salt
2 cakes (0.6 oz.) compressed fresh yeast or 2 packages active-dry yeast	*1¼ cups (2½ sticks) butter, chilled*
4 cups plus 2 tablespoons white bread flour	*¾ cup warm milk (105° to 115°F)*
	1 egg, beaten

Put the water into a small bowl. Crumble or sprinkle in the yeast. Leave fresh yeast 5 minutes and dry 15 minutes.

Put the flour into a large mixing bowl. Toss in the sugar and salt. Rub in ¼ cup (½ stick) of the butter. Make a well in the center and pour in the yeast liquid and the milk. Mix to a dough. Turn onto a floured work surface and knead until smooth. Return the dough to the bowl and cover with plastic wrap. Put the dough into the refrigerator 1 hour.

Put the remaining butter into a large plastic bag or between 2 pieces of plastic wrap. Pound with a rolling pin until it makes a flat 9- x 5-inch rectangle. Knead the dough and roll it into an 18- x 10-inch rectangle. Place the rectangle of butter in the center of the dough. Fold over the ends of the dough and then the sides. Roll the package lengthwise into a rectangle and then fold it into thirds. Put the folded dough in a plastic bag or wrap in plastic wrap. Return to the refrigerator 10 minutes. Roll and chill 3 more times.

After the final chilling, roll the dough into a square about ¼ inch thick. Cut it into twelve 6-inch equilateral triangles. Using a rolling pin, roll each triangle from base to tip to elongate slightly. Gently pull out the corners of the base so they stick out. Roll up the triangle from the base to the tip. Place the rolled dough on a floured cookie sheet so the tip is underneath. Bring the ends around to make a crescent shape.

Leave the croissants uncovered to rise 30 minutes. Meanwhile, heat the oven to 400°F.

Just before baking the croissants, glaze them with the beaten egg. Bake 15 minutes, or until they are golden brown; they will rise in the oven and the tip will pull itself out to lie across the top. Cool the croissants on wire racks, and serve them just warm.

Variations

For added variety, croissants can be filled with small amounts of sweet or savory ingredients. Place the fillings on the bottom half of the croissant before rolling. Only small amounts are needed.

Chocolate Croissants

You need thin pieces of chocolate only, so carefully cut a bar of bittersweet chocolate into thin strips. Place the strips of chocolate lengthwise across the bottom of the dough triangle before rolling up.

Almond Croissants

Mix 4 tablespoons ground blanched almonds with 1 tablespoon honey and a few drops of almond extract. Put 2 teaspoons on the bottom of each triangle before rolling up.

Apple Croissants

Put 1 tablespoon puréed apple on the bottom of each triangle before rolling up.

Cheese Croissants

Put 1 tablespoon grated Gruyère cheese on the bottom of each triangle before rolling up.

Cheese and Ham Croissants

Put 1 tablespoon grated cheese and 1 tablespoon finely chopped lean cooked ham on the bottom of each triangle before rolling up.

Kugelhupf

For more than 500 years, the Viennese have had a reputation for making fine bread, yeasted cakes, and pastries. They like to gather in coffeehouses morning or afternoon to enjoy a wide variety of sweet treats.

One of the most traditional yeasted cakes is the Viennese kugelhupf. Cookbooks have a number of spellings, including "kugelhopf" and "gugelkopf," but they all mean the same thing: a rich, sweet, yeasted cake, baked in a fluted, decorated mold.

A kugelhupf can be plain or can contain nuts, dried fruit, or candied peel. The dough can be flavored with almond, lemon, or vanilla, or part of it may be mixed with chocolate to produce a marbled effect. A kugelhupf is usually sprinkled liberally with confectioners' sugar when cool.

Emperor Franz Joseph I of Austria fell in love with Frau Katherina Schratt, an actress at the Burg Theater. He visited her every day at 4.30 p.m., when she would be taking from the oven the small, individual kugelhupf he was so fond of.

The kugelhupf has another claim to fame. Marie Antoinette's mother was Austrian, and the young queen had a particular liking for the cake of her ancestral country. When, just before the French Revolution, she suggested the starving peasants eat cake instead of bread, she was referring to kugelhupf.

SALLY LUNN

The Sally Lunn is a rich bread, usually round, which is served split crosswise and thickly buttered. The name is probably a corruption of the French *soleil et lune* ("sun and moon") sometimes shortened to *solileme*, the name for a similar bread in France. In England, the name became Sally Lunn, and a legend grew up about a lady of the same name who sold homemade cakes from a store in Bath in the eighteenth century.

Sally Lunn bread has a very light, almost cakelike texture, a thin crisp crust, and a golden crumb. Made without extra flavorings, it can be served either with preserves or with cheese. The lemon peel and candied peel are nineteenth-century additions to give the loaf more of a tea-cake flavor. Although rich, a Sally Lunn is quick to make because there is only one rising time.

MAKES ONE LOAF

4 tablespoons warm water (105° to 115°F)	2 tablespoons chopped candied peel (optional)
1 teaspoon sugar	2 eggs, beaten
1 cake (0.6 oz.) compressed fresh yeast or 1 package active-dry yeast	½ cup heavy cream
butter for greasing	4 tablespoons milk
1⅔ cups white bread flour	GLAZE
½ teaspoon salt	1 tablespoon each sugar and milk
grated peel of ½ lemon (optional)	

Put the water into a small bowl and stir in the sugar. Crumble or sprinkle in the yeast. Leave fresh yeast 5 minutes and dry 15 minutes. Butter a 7-inch deep cake pan.

Put the flour into a large mixing bowl. Add the salt and the lemon peel and/or the candied peel if you are using. Make a well in the center and pour in the yeast liquid, eggs, cream, and milk. Knead the mixture with your hand to make a very moist dough.

Transfer the dough to the prepared pan and leave in a warm place for about 30 minutes, or until it doubles in volume.

Meanwhile, heat the oven to 400°F. Bake 30 minutes, or until it is risen and golden brown. For the glaze, dissolve the sugar in the milk. Brush it over the top of the baked loaf and put the loaf back into the oven 1 minute for the glaze to dry. Cool the loaf in the pan 5 minutes, then unmold and transfer to a wire rack 10 minutes longer.

To serve, cut the loaf into 3 horizontal slices, spread each piece thickly with butter, and then sandwich the pieces back together. Cut the loaf into thin vertical slices; serve with preserves or cheese or as an accompaniment to fruit compotes.

Salami, Cheese, *and* Onion Tart

This rich tart has a bread-dough crust, similar to the style of tarts made in Switzerland. The filling should sink into the crust, making the center moist and full of flavor with a crisp edge. Serve the tart warm as a light meal or at room temperature for snacks and picnics.

MAKES ONE 10-INCH TART

¾ cup warm water (105° to 115°F)

1 cake (0.6 oz.) compressed fresh yeast or 1 package active-dry yeast

1¾ cups plus 2 tablespoons white bread flour

1 teaspoon salt

4 tablespoons butter, cut into small pieces and softened

FILLING

2 onions

2 tablespoons butter

2 eggs

⅔ cup light cream

4 tablespoons milk

2 ounces Italian salami, diced

9 ounces Gruyère cheese, grated

Put the water into a large mixing bowl. Crumble or sprinkle in the yeast. Leave fresh yeast 5 minutes and dry 15 minutes. Mix together the flour and salt. Add them to the yeast liquid. Begin to mix them in and then add the butter. Mix to a dough. Turn the dough onto a floured work surface and knead until it is smooth. Return the dough to the bowl. Cover it with a clean dish towel and leave in a warm place 1 hour, or until it doubles in volume.

To make the filling, thinly slice the onions. Soften them in the butter. Beat the eggs with the cream and milk.

Knead the dough again and roll it into a circle large enough to line a 10-inch tart pan with a removable bottom. Sprinkle half the cheese, half the salami, and all the onions over. Add the remaining cheese and salami. Pour in the egg and cream mixture.

Leave the tart for 20 minutes in a warm place. Meanwhile, heat the oven to 400°F. Bake 20 minutes, or until the top of the filling is golden. Remove tart from pan as soon as it is baked. Serve warm or leave it to cool completely, on a wire rack.

Sorrows of Werther

"Werther had a love for Charlotte
Such as words could never utter;
Would you know how first he met her?
She was cutting bread and butter."

WILLIAM MAKEPEACE THACKERAY,
1811–1863

63

SUN-DRIED TOMATO BREAD

Since the recent popularity of sun-dried tomatoes, different types of tomato bread have been appearing in bakeries and supermarkets. There isn't a classic recipe for this, but most are made with white flour and enriched with olive oil and an egg.

MAKES 14 ROLLS

¾ cup warm water (105° to 115°F)
1 cake (0.6 oz.) compressed fresh yeast or 1 package active-dry yeast
4 ounces sun-dried tomatoes packed in oil
2½ cups white bread flour
1 teaspoon salt

1 tablespoon chopped fresh oregano, or 1 teaspoon dried oregano
1 teaspoon chopped fresh thyme, or 1 teaspoon dried thyme
1 egg, beaten
4 tablespoons olive oil

Put the water into a small bowl. Crumble and sprinkle in the yeast. Leave fresh yeast 5 minutes and dry 15 minutes. Drain and finely chop the sun-dried tomatoes.

Put the flour into a bowl. Stir in the salt and herbs. Make a well in the center. Pour in the yeast liquid and the egg. Mix to a dough. Turn the dough onto a floured work surface and knead until it is smooth. Gradually knead in the olive oil, about 1 tablespoon at a time. Divide the dough into 2 pieces. Knead the tomatoes into one piece only; put the pieces of dough into separate bowls. Cover them with clean dish towels and leave them in a warm place 1 hour, or until they doubles in volume.

Oil a deep 8-inch cake pan. Knead each piece of dough separately and divide it into 8 small balls, to make 16 in total. Arrange the pieces in a checkerboard pattern in the pan. Leave the pan in a warm place 20 minutes for the rolls to rise. Meanwhile, heat the oven to 400°F.

Bake 25 minutes, or until the rolls are firm and sound hollow when tapped on the bottom but has not browned. Turn the loaf out onto a wire rack to cool. To eat, pull off the herb-flavored and tomato rolls separately.

65

Danish Pastries

Danish pastries are made in many parts of the world and are known by a variety of names. All have light, flaky pastry, while the shapes and fillings vary.

Folding and rolling the chilled dough is an essential step in the making of light and flaky Danish pastries.

Copenhagen is thought to be the city where Danish pastries were first made.

Danish pastries are made with light, flaky pastry, elaborately shaped, filled with just enough sweet filling, and topped with a little frosting. While English-speaking countries call them Danish pastries, the Danish call them *Wienebrot* (Vienna bread) and the Germans *Kopenhagener* (from Copenhagen). Like many such delicacies, their origins are disputed.

One story maintains, in the nineteenth century, the bakers of Copenhagen went on strike and demanded cash wages instead of their customary room and board. They were all fired and were replaced by bakers from Germany and Austria, whose expertise was in making sweet, yeasted cakes.

The other, usually more accepted, explanation goes back to the sixteenth century, when a young French baker by the name of Claudius Gelée was making brioches and forgot to add the butter. When his master came in, he quickly folded the dough over the telltale butter lying on the countertop. He then kept rolling and folding until all the butter had been incorporated into the dough. When he baked the dough, the surprise result was flaky pastry. Using his serendipitous discovery, Claudius Gelée opened his own bakery in Paris. He was later invited to Florence by two Italian bakers, brothers by the name of Mosca.

The Mosca brothers took the recipe several stages forward by developing different shapes and fillings, and it was not long before the pastries were also being made across the border in Austria.

Enter two young Danish bakers (their names have never been discovered) who traveled to Vienna to learn the secrets of good baking and who eventually took their new-found

Basic Recipe for Danish Pastries

Makes about 30 pastries

1¼ cups milk
14 tablespoons (1¼ sticks) butter, chilled
2 tablespoons sugar
1 egg
1 egg yolk
2½ cakes (0.6 oz.) compressed fresh yeast
3⅓ cups white bread flour
½ teaspoon salt
¼ teaspoon ground cardamom

Put the milk, 2 tablespoons of the butter, and all the sugar into a saucepan and heat over low heat. Stir until the butter melts and the sugar dissolves; cool to lukewarm. Beat in the egg and egg yolk. Crumble in the yeast. Put the flour into a bowl and toss in the salt and cardamom. Make a well in the center and pour in the yeast liquid. Mix to a dough.

Turn the dough onto a floured work surface and knead until it is smooth. Form the dough into a cube shape, put it into a plastic bag, and chill it in the refrigerator 30 minutes.

Put the remaining butter between 2 pieces of plastic wrap and hit it with a rolling pin into an 8- x 4-inch rectangle. Take the dough out and roll into a 16- x 8-inch rectangle. Place the butter in the center and fold the sides of the dough over it. Roll out the dough to a rectangle ¾ inch thick. Fold the dough into 3 portions, return it to the plastic bag, and put it into the refrigerator 10 minutes. Repeat this rolling, folding, and chilling 3 more times.

After the final chilling, roll out the dough and fold it as before. Cut it crosswise into 3 pieces. It is now ready to be made into pastries of various shapes and with a choice of fillings.

To bake, lay the pastries on floured cookie sheets and leave them in a warm place 20 minutes to rise. Meanwhile, heat the oven to 400°F. Bake 20 minutes, or until they are golden brown. Cool on wire racks.

knowledge home with them to Denmark. In Denmark, the pastries are mostly eaten with coffee.

Today, Danish pastries are made in many parts of the world, but there are still two specialties, produced with the same dough, that are made only in Denmark. One is Butter Cake, baked in a round cake pan and consisting of a circle of dough topped with more dough made into circles, spirals, or other elaborate shapes, the center of which is then filled with a mixture of butter, sugar, and golden raisins. The other is the *Julekage* or "Yule Cake," decorated with a star and filled with spiced, sweet custard, raisins, and candied peel. Millions of *Julekage* are sold in the weeks running up to Christmas.

Danish Pastry Fillings

Each is enough for one-third of the dough (see recipe on left).

Spiced Golden Raisin Filling

2 tablespoons superfine sugar
1 teaspoon ground cinnamon
2 tablespoons butter, softened
2 tablespoons golden raisins

Beat the sugar and cinnamon into the butter. Fold in the golden raisins.

Almond Filling

½ cup finely ground blanched almonds
⅓ cup superfine sugar
1 tablespoon beaten egg
3 drops almond extract

Mix together the ground almonds and sugar in a bowl. Bind them together with the egg. Beat in the almond extract.

Custard Cream Filling

1 egg yolk
1 tablespoon all-purpose flour
1 teaspoon cornstarch
1 tablespoon sugar
⅔ cup milk
3 drops vanilla extract

Beat the egg yolk lightly in a bowl and work in the flour, cornstarch, sugar, and 4 tablespoons of the milk. Put the remaining milk into a saucepan and bring to just below boiling point. Gradually stir the hot milk into the yolk mixture. Return the mixture to the saucepan and stir over low heat to make a thick custard. Remove from the heat and beat in the vanilla extract. Cool the mixture completely before using.

Decoration

The pastries can be served plain or drizzled with a simple frosting made from ½ cup confectioners' sugar and a little water. Halved candied cherries, chopped nuts, or slivered almonds can be sprinkled on top.

Some Danish Pastry Shapes

Here are some suggestions for shaping your pastries.

Snails

Roll out the dough into a ¾-inch-thick rectangle. Spread evenly with the filling. Roll up the dough along one long side and cut it into 1-inch thick slices. Place the slices on a floured cookie sheet.

Cock's Combs

Roll out the dough into an 8-inch rectangle. Spread half the width with the filling. Fold over the other half and cut the folded dough into 4-inch squares. Make 3 cuts in the folded side of the dough, from the fold to within ½ inch of the opposite side. Place the pastries on a floured cookie sheet and gently spread out the sections.

Pinwheels

Roll out the dough to a thickness of ¾ inch and cut into 6-inch squares. Cut from each corner to within ½ inch of the center. Put a portion of the filling in the center. Fold alternate sections to the middle so the points slightly overlap. Seal the points by gently pressing down in the center.
Directions for forming crescents, envelopes, and twists are given in the section on bread shapes on page 32.

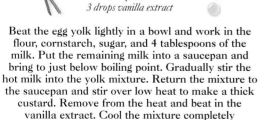

BLACKBERRY BREAD

In English cottages, blackberry bread was made in the fall, the wild blackberries being a cost-free substitute for expensive currants or raisins. Whole-wheat flour was produced with the wheat gained from gleaning in the harvest fields. The bread is semisweet, moist, spicy, and streaked with purple from the blackberries. It is excellent, buttered, in a lunchbox or as an afternoon snack.

MAKES ONE LARGE LOAF

¾ cup warm water (105˚ to 115˚F)
2 cakes (0.6 oz.) compressed fresh yeast or 2 packages active-dry yeast
3⅓ cups whole-wheat flour
½ teaspoon salt
½ teaspoon ground cinnamon
¼ teaspoon freshly grated nutmeg
1 egg, beaten
⅔ cup warm milk (105˚ to 115˚F)
2 tablespoons honey
3 tablespoons butter, cut into small pieces and softened
1¾ cups blackberries, fresh, or frozen and just thawed

Put the water into a small bowl. Crumble or sprinkle in the yeast. Leave fresh yeast 5 minutes and dry 15 minutes.

Put the flour into a large mixing bowl and stir in the salt, cinnamon, and nutmeg. Make a well in the center and add the yeast liquid, egg, milk, honey, and butter. Mix to a moist dough. Add the blackberries and carefully stir them in. Knead the dough in the bowl, taking care not to squash the blackberries too much. Cover the dough with a clean dish towel and leave in a warm place 1 hour, or until it doubles.

Meanwhile, heat the oven to 400°F. Turn the dough onto a floured work surface and knead it again. Form it into a loaf shape and put it into a 9- x 5- x 2½-inch bread pan.

Bake 40 minutes, or until the loaf sounds hollow when tapped on the bottom and the top is just browned. Transfer to a wire rack to cool.

CHRISTMAS FRUIT BREAD

This is a whole-wheat version of the German Christmas specialty called the *Dresdner stollen*. It is fruity and spicy, and good to serve sliced for something to nibble on Christmas Day.

MAKES ONE LARGE LOAF

½ cup warm water (105˚ to 115˚F)
2 cakes (0.6 oz.) compressed fresh yeast or 2 packages active-dry yeast
3⅓ cups whole-wheat flour
1 teaspoon salt
⅓ cup dark brown sugar
1 teaspoon apple-pie spice
¾ cup warm milk (105˚ to 115˚F)
1 egg, beaten
6 tablespoons butter, cut into small pieces and softened
½ cup raisins
½ cup golden raisins
⅓ cup chopped candied peel
4 tablespoons slivered almonds
2 tablespoons confectioners' sugar, sifted

Put the water into a small bowl. Crumble and sprinkle in the yeast. Leave fresh yeast 5 minutes and dry 15 minutes.

Put the flour into a bowl and stir in the salt, sugar, and apple-pie spice. Make a well in the center and pour in the yeast liquid and the milk. Add the egg and butter and mix to a dough. Turn the dough out onto a floured work surface and knead until it is smooth. Gently knead in the dried fruit, candied peel, and almonds.

Return the dough to the bowl. Cover it with a clean dish towel and leave it in a warm place 1 hour, or until doubled.

Knead the dough again. Roll it into a 12- x 8-inch rectangle. Fold the dough into three along the long sides. Place it on a floured baking sheet, seam side down. With your hands, taper the ends of the loaf into points.

Leave the loaf in a warm place 1 hour, or until it doubles in volume. Meanwhile, heat the oven to 400°F. Bake 40 minutes, or until the loaf sounds hollow when tapped on the bottom and is a good brown color. Transfer to a wire rack to cool. When it has just cooled, coat it with the sugar.

Panettoni

The panettoni originated in Lombardy, one of the richest regions in Italy, where butter rather than olive oil is the main cooking ingredient. This is a rich, yeasted cake, with a dome-shaped top said to resemble the cupolas of Lombardy churches. It is light in texture, yellow, and contains golden raisins and candied peel.

The panettoni is the food most often associated with Milan, the principal city of Lombardy. It is sold in most of the food stores and even at the windows of trains stopping in the main station. It was originally a Christmas treat but is now available at all times of the year. It can be eaten at any time of the day, although it is particularly popular with coffee at breakfast.

The legend of the origin of panettoni explains its name, which was once "pan de Tonio," meaning "Tony's bread." Tonio was a baker who lived in the quarter of Milan known as Borogo delle Grazie in the fifteenth century, and had a beautiful daughter named Adalgisa.

A rich and well-connected young man, Ughetto della Tela, courted Adalgisa, but Ughetto's family would not

accept her because her father was a tradesman. However, Ughetto discerned that it was not breeding that his father was looking for, but money, so he hatched a plan. Just before Christmas, Ughetto sold his hunting falcons to buy the baker flour, eggs, and butter to make the traditional cakes of the region. He also added his own special touch, golden raisins and candied lemon peel.

Tonio set about making his cakes. They were so good everyone came to buy them, and soon he was rich enough for Ughetto's family to accept Adalgisa.

SHEEP CHEESE *and* ONION BREAD

This is a variation of a German recipe, the original of which gave double the quantities here. The original recipe would have used a local sheep milk cheese, but feta makes a good substitute. The amounts given below produce a large, well-risen, oval loaf that is a meal in itself. The addition of the chopped raw onion might appear strange, but it steams gently in the heat of the baking dough and softens. The pieces of cheese melt, leaving the bread with a holey texture, a soft crumb, and a delicious cheese flavor. Butter is optional and a crisp salad or a vegetable soup is all you need to make a satisfying meal.

MAKES ONE LARGE LOAF

1½ cups warm water (105° to 115°F)
2 cakes (0.6 oz.) compressed fresh yeast or 2 packages active-dry yeast
1 large onion

4 ounces feta or other similar sheep-milk cheese
3⅓ cups white bread flour
2 teaspoons salt
1 tablespoon olive or sunflower oil

Put one-third of the water into a large mixing bowl. Crumble or sprinkle in the yeast. Leave fresh yeast 5 minutes and dry 15 minutes.

Finely chop the onion and the cheese. Mix the flour and salt together.

Add the remaining water to the yeast liquid. Stir in the flour mixture followed by the onion and cheese. Mix together to form a dough. Turn the dough onto a floured work surface and knead until it is smooth. Return the dough to the bowl. Cover it with a clean dish towel and leave in a warm place 1 hour, or until it doubles in volume.

Knead the dough again and form it into an oval shape about 10 inches long; place on a floured cookie sheet. Brush the surface with the oil and make 3 diagonal slashes on the top. Meanwhile, heat the oven to 400°F. Leave the loaf in a warm place 20 minutes to rise.

Bake 35 minutes, or until the top is golden brown and the bottom sounds hollow when tapped. Transfer to a wire rack to cool.

SHRIMP *and* BEANSPROUT BUNS

Bread does not feature very much in the Chinese diet except in Canton, where the specialty is the *dim sum* meal, eaten as a snack either in the middle of the morning or the afternoon, usually at a local *dim sum* restaurant. *Dim sum* means "to please the heart," and the meal should be an enjoyable treat. Chinese buns are made with a soft, plain dough formed around a sweet or savory filling, and steamed in a bamboo steamer. The dough does not have any salt, so it has a slightly sweet flavor. The recipe below makes an excellent snack or one of several dishes in a Chinese meal.

MAKES 12 BUNS

4 tablespoons warm water (105° to 115°F)	4 scallions
2 cakes (0.6 oz.) compressed fresh yeast or 2 packages active-dry yeast	4 tablespoons sunflower oil
	1 garlic clove, finely chopped
	4 ounces tiny shelled cooked shrimp
2 teaspoons sugar	1 cup beansprouts
3⅓ cups white bread flour	2 tablespoons soy sauce
1¼ cups warm milk (105° to 115°F)	2 tablespoons dry sherry (optional)
½ ounce fresh gingerroot	

To make the dough, put the warm water into a small bowl. Crumble or sprinkle in the yeast and sugar. Leave fresh yeast 5 minutes and dry 15 minutes.

Put the flour into a mixing bowl and make a well in the center. Pour in the yeast liquid and the milk and mix to a dough. Turn the dough onto a floured board and knead until it is smooth. Return the dough to the bowl. Cover it with a clean dish towel and leave in a warm place 1 hour to double in volume. Punch down the dough firmly with your fist, cover it again, and leave 30 minutes longer, or until doubles in volume.

To make the filling, peel and grate the ginger. Chop the scallions. Heat the oil in a skillet over high heat. Add the ginger, scallions, and garlic and stir-fry 30 seconds. Add the shrimp and stir-fry 30 seconds longer. Add the beansprouts and stir-fry 2 minutes, or until they wilt. Stir in the soy sauce and sherry and let them bubble until reduced by half. Take the pan off the heat and cool the contents.

Knead the dough again and cut it into 12 pieces. Roll each piece into a 4-inch circle. Put a portion of the filling in the center of each circle. Gather up the edge of each circle so each side meets at the top and twist around to secure. Put

the buns onto a floured work surface. Cover them with a clean dish towel and leave 30 minutes to rise.

Bring some water to boil under a large steamer. Put in as many buns as the steamer will hold, leaving a space of about 1 inch around each one. Cover the buns and steam 10 minutes; cook the remainder in the same way. If the buns have to be steamed in 2 or more batches, put the ones steamed first on top of the ones still steaming for the last 2 minutes of cooking time, so they can all be served hot.

ANCHOVY BREAD

This sourdough-type of bread flavored with anchovies is a specialty of Provence in France. This variation is rich and well flavored, and excellent served, unbuttered, with casseroles and stews.

MAKES ONE LARGE LOAF

¾ cup warm water (105° to 115°F)
1 cake (0.6 oz.) compressed fresh yeast or 1 package active-day yeast
3⅓ cups white bread flour

1 teaspoon salt
2 cans (1½ oz.) anchovy fillets in oil
4 tablespoons butter, softened
2 eggs, beaten

Put the water into a large mixing bowl. Crumble or sprinkle in the yeast. Leave fresh yeast 5 minutes and dry yeast 15 minutes.

Add half the flour and all the salt. Mix to a dough. Turn the dough onto a floured work surface and knead until it is smooth. Return it to the bowl. Cover with plastic wrap and leave in a warm place 2 days.

Drain and mash the anchovies. Leaving the dough in the bowl, knead in the butter and then the eggs, a little at a time; it will take at least 10 minutes for them both to be incorporated. Knead in the remaining flour. Turn the dough onto a work surface and knead until it is smooth. Return to the bowl again, cover it with a dish towel and leave in a warm place 1 hour, or until it doubles in volume.

Knead the dough again, form it into a ball, and place it on a floured cookie sheet. Leave the dough in a warm place 20 minutes to rise. Meanwhile, heat the oven to 400°F.

Bake 25 minutes, or until the top is golden brown and the bottom sounds hollow when tapped. Transfer to a wire rack to cool.

CHEESE-FILLED ROLLS

These buns are based on a Russian recipe called *khachapuri*. The original recipe would have used a local sheep-milk cheese, but feta makes a good substitute. The buns are made from a plain bread dough, which encloses a savory cheese filling. The buns make ideal fare for lunchboxes and picnics.

MAKES 16 ROLLS

⅔ cup warm milk (105° to 115°F)
1 cake (0.6 oz.) compressed fresh yeast or 1 package active-dry yeast
4 tablespoons butter, softened
1¾ cups plus 2 tablespoons white bread flour

1 teaspoon salt
FILLING
1½ cups grated feta cheese
1 egg, beaten
4 tablespoons chopped fresh parsley or cilantro

To make the dough, put the milk into a large mixing bowl. Crumble and sprinkle in the yeast. Leave fresh yeast 5 minutes and dry 15 minutes.

Add the butter to the milk and yeast liquid. Stir in the flour and salt and knead to a dough. Turn the dough onto a floured work surface and knead until it is smooth. Return the dough to the bowl. Cover with a clean dish towel and leave in a warm place 1 hour, or until it doubles in volume.

To make the filling, combine the cheese, egg, and herb.

Knead the dough again and divide it into 16 even-size pieces. Roll each piece into a 5-inch circle. Place a portion of the filling in the center of each circle. Fold in 2 opposite sides of each circle to just touch in the center. Fold in the 2 remaining sides in the same way. Pinch the corners to seal. Put the buns onto floured cookie sheets and leave them in a warm place 20 minutes to rise. Meanwhile, heat the oven to 400°F.

Bake 20 minutes, or until the rolls are just brown. Cool them on wire racks. Either eat warm or at room temperature.

71

Advertising and Packaging

For thousands of years bread, like other goods, was sold and advertised by a variety of direct methods in the streets, fairs and markets. It was not until newspapers and magazines became more widely available that advertising took on its modern guise.

Ever since bread was baked commercially, bakers have been finding ways to ensure that their loaves came to the public eye and were bought by the most customers.

Before the nineteenth century and the widespread availability of written material, it was common to see people carrying trays of goods through the streets, calling out to passers-by to come and sample their wares. People would come from their houses when they heard the cries and take their pick. The baker who shouted loudest, or who had the cleverest turn of phrase, would always sell the most. This is the origin of the old street cries, some of which have been handed down in the form of nursery rhymes such as:

This advertisement for Everfresh Bread gives the impression that it was eaten by royalty - a sure selling point in nineteenth century Britain.

"Hot cross buns,
Hot cross buns,
One a penny,
Two a penny,
Hot cross buns.
If you have no daughters
Give them to your sons.
One a penny,
Two a penny,
Hot cross buns."

Another popular method of attracting customers was for the baker to display his wares outside his store. People in a crowded street market or fairground would look for a loaf of bread impaled on a pole standing high above the heads of shoppers and the frames of stalls.

Around the beginning of the nineteenth century bakers began to switch from handmade loaves to machine-made bread. There was little difference between any of the standard loaves on sale and so the difference had to be in the promotion. As more people became literate and newspapers and magazines became more readily available, advertising, as we know it, began and copywriters started their ever-increasing search for the perfect slogan.

In Britain, for example, S. Fitton and Son, millers of Macclesfield, began to promote Hovis flour for breadmaking. Their campaign was based around the fact that their product was "Supplied to The Queen and Royal Family." In the patriotic days of Queen Victoria and Empire, that was a great selling point in itself. However, their advertisements also proclaimed that: "1 1/2lb Hovis Bread is more nourishing than 1/2 lb Beef Steak," and "Absolutely Necessary for all growing children." Hovis bread advertisements

Advertisers have always focused on the health benefits of bread. In Britain, during the early part of this century, many children were undernourished, so this claim would would have appealed to many mothers.

In the 1800s, American companies began marketing specialty flours to home breadmakers

appeared in numerous magazines, and, in addition, nearly every small baker and grocer in the country had a metal sign, bearing the one word, "Hovis," fixed on the outside of their store. These signs have now become collector's items and museum pieces.

In America, sliced bread was first marketed on a commercial scale in 1928, soon after the first commercial bread slicer was installed in Missouri. Before that unsliced bread was sold commercially, but the vast majority of people bought their bread from neighborhood grocers and door-to-door pushcart vendors. Once sliced bread was available in packaging, it didn't take long for its marketing to catch up.

Initially, some bakers resisted the introduction of wrapping. This was particularly true of Australian bakers who were "unanimously opposed on the grounds of cost, uncertainty of hygeienic benefit and total lack of public demand." However, by 1928 three Sydney bakers were wrapping, and others soon followed.

After the Second World War, the sliced, wrapped loaf became increasingly popular, and this was a golden opportunity for manufacturers to give their loaves fancy names and eye-catching wrappers bearing distinctive logos. One of the most widely recognized trademarks in the American food industry is Miss Sunbeam, the symbol for Sunbeam bread, created in 1942 for the Quality Bakers of America. Inspired by a little girl playing in a park in New York City, the sweet blond child doubled sales in just 13 weeks and the spin-off into promotional dolls and toys had a huge response.

In Britain, there was Wonder Bread, which "Helps Build Bodies Twelve Ways," and Taystee enriched bread, "with wholesome good taste." Both these advertising campaigns relied on promoting the nutritional quality of

the loaves in question - a claim that has been the underlying theme of most bread advertisements for the last fifty years.

Promotion was not restricted to bread, manufacturers also wanted to advertise bread-making ingredients to both commercial and home bakers. In 1880, for example, the Washburn Crosby company of Minneapolis, Minnesota, (forerunner of General Mills) entered its flour in the first Millers' International Exhibition and took the bronze, silver and gold medals. From then on, the company's highest quality flour has been mrketed under the Good Medal brand.

Today's shoppers are presented with a vast range of bread-making products and breads, making brand loyalty an important issue for companies. Advertising has never been more important.

Even plain, uncut loaves can be given an eye-catching wrapper which promotes the brand name and logo and also gives nutritional information.

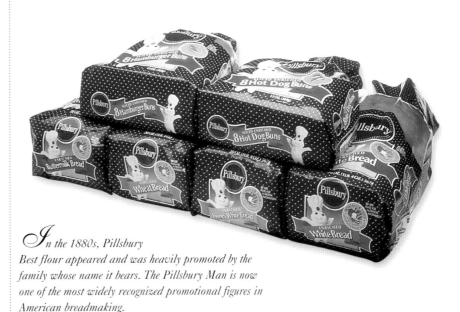

In the 1880s, Pillsbury Best flour appeared and was heavily promoted by the family whose name it bears. The Pillsbury Man is now one of the most widely recognized promotional figures in American breadmaking.

DOUGH CAKE

Dough cake is another traditional bread from rural England. When large batches of bread were made at home, a small portion of the dough was set aside to be rolled and layered with sugar, spices, dried fruit, and fat. Eaten warm, it is an old-fashioned teatime treat—moist, sweet, and spicy—and with the layers still visible, adding interest to the texture. Whole-wheat flour gives a nostalgic, country flavor.

MAKES ONE 10-INCH LOAF

Basic Loaf Dough (page 30) made with 3⅓ cups white bread flour or whole wheat bread flour
12 tablespoons butter
½ cup plus 2 tablespoons soft brown sugar
4 tablespoons dried currants
4 tablespoons raisins
1 teaspoon apple-pie spice
GLAZE
1 tablespoon sugar dissolved in 1 tablespoon water

Make up the bread dough (see page 30) and leave it to rise 1 hour.

Knead the dough on a floured work surface. Roll it out into a rectangle about ½ inch thick. Spread 2 tablespoons of the butter on two-thirds of the dough and fold the dough into three, like folding a letter. Roll out the dough again. Spread with a quarter of the remaining butter. Mix together the sugar, dried fruit, and spice. Sprinkle a quarter of the mixture over the dough. Fold the dough into three. Repeat the process 3 times, using one-third of the butter and 1 tablespoon each of currants and raisins each time, the last time folding the dough but not rolling it out again.

Place the folded dough in a 10- x 8-inch baking pan (do not use a cookie sheet because the butter sometimes runs out during baking.) Leave in a warm place 15 minutes to rise. Meanwhile, heat the oven to 400°F.

Bake 40 minutes, or until it is golden brown and sounds hollow when tapped on the bottom. Brush it with the glaze and return it to the oven 1 minute. Transfer to a wire rack to cool a little. If possible, eat it warm.

CHELSEA BUNS

Chelsea buns were first made in the early part of the nineteenth century in The Old Chelsea Bun House off the Pimlico Road in London. The proprietor was Mr. Richard Hand, who ran the establishment with his family and who was known as Captain Bun. Crowds of people would travel from the city to the Bun House at weekends to taste the rich, sweet, sticky buns hot from the oven. Even King George III and Queen Charlotte were regularly seen there. The Old Chelsea Bun House burned down in 1839, but fortunately Chelsea buns have been made ever since.

MAKES 12 BUNS

⅔ cup warm milk (105° to 115°F)
2 cakes (0.6 oz.) compressed fresh yeast or 2 packages active-dry yeast
4¼ cups plus 2 tablespoons white bread flour
½ teaspoon salt
1 cup superfine sugar
4 eggs, beaten
14 tablespoons (1¾ sticks) butter, softened
1½ cups currants
1 teaspoon apple-pie spice
GLAZE
¼ cup sugar boiled with 2 tablespoons water

Put the milk into a small bowl. Crumble or sprinkle in the yeast. Leave fresh yeast 5 minutes and dry 15 minutes.

Put the flour into a bowl. Stir in the salt and half the sugar. Make a well in the center. Add the yeast liquid, the eggs, and half the butter. Mix to a dough. Turn out onto a floured work surface and knead until it is smooth. Return the dough to the bowl. Cover with a clean dish towel and leave it in a warm place 1 hour, or until it doubles in volume.

Knead the dough again and roll into a square about ½ inch thick. Spread with the remaining butter and sprinkle on half the remaining sugar. Fold the dough into thirds, like folding a letter, and roll it out again. Sprinkle with the remaining sugar and all the currants and spice. Roll it up like a jelly roll. Cut the roll into 12 slices, each 1½ inches thick. Place the slices close together, but not quite touching, on a floured cookie sheet. Leave them 20 minutes to rise, by which time they should be touching. Meanwhile, heat the oven to 400°F.

Bake 20 minutes, or until the buns are golden brown. Brush with the prepared glaze and return to the oven 2 minutes for the glaze to dry. Cool the buns on wire racks, still joined together. Pull them apart just before serving.

CHAPTER THREE

FLAT BREADS

Flat breads are made all over the world. Some are eaten as snacks, many are used to accompany meals, and others serve as both food and eating utensil combined. The enormous variety of textures and shapes makes them an exciting accompaniment to any meal.

FLAT BREADS

The very earliest breads were unleavened and baked flat on hot stones, and many flat breads enjoyed today are still made the same way. There are soft, flexible chapatis and tasty tortillas for wrapping around food, as well as more substantial parathas, flavored with spice, or crispy knackebrods and crispbreads from Scandinavia, ideal to serve with cheese. Adding yeast, or another leavening agent, makes a thicker, puffier dough, even when it is rolled flat for baking.

Nan bread is rolled into oval shapes while pita bread forms a handy pocket to hold a variety of ingredients. Topped with herbs and sesame seeds and baked in rounds, flat bread becomes a favorite Middle Eastern snack called mannaeesh. Italian focaccia accompanies cheese, salads, or cooked dishes, and the apple and walnut streusel cake from Germany makes a hearty dessert. For a traditional English tea, nothing can beat warm, buttery crumpets and griddle scones.

From sowing to loaf, *19th century*

79

MANNAEESH

These breads are a variation of ones so popular in the Lebanon. There they traditionally have a strongly flavored topping made with large amounts of herbs combined with sesame seeds. The smaller amounts of fresh herbs used in this recipe gives a milder flavor more suited to Western palates. *Mannaeesh* are eaten for breakfast, with tea or coffee, but are also excellent with soups and salads. They are soft and very light.

MAKES 10 SMALL, ROUND BREADS

1¼ cups warm water (105° to 115°F)
1 cake (0.6 oz.) compressed fresh yeast or 1 package active-dry yeast
2 tablespoons olive oil
3½ cups white bread flour
½ teaspoon salt

TOPPING
6 tablespoons olive oil
4 tablespoons chopped fresh thyme
4 tablespoons chopped fresh marjoram
3 tablespoons sesame seeds

Put the water into a large mixing bowl. Crumble or sprinkle in the yeast. Leave fresh yeast 5 minutes and dry 15 minutes. Stir in the oil. Stir in the flour and salt. Form the mixture into a dough. Turn out onto a floured work surface and knead well. Return the dough to the bowl and cover with a clean dish towel. Leave in a warm place 1 hour, or until it doubles in volume.

Knead the dough for a second time and divide it into 10 equal pieces. Roll each piece into a flat circle, about 5 inches across. Place them on a floured work surface and leave them 20 minutes to rise. Cover 4 cookie sheets with aluminum foil and put them into the oven to heat. Meanwhile, heat the oven to 450°F. Mix together the topping ingredients.

Spread the topping mixture evenly over each dough circle. Place on the hot cookie sheets. Bake 8 minutes, or until the breads is cooked through but still soft and white. Transfer to wire racks to cool.

BUCKWHEAT BREAD

In the Baltic states, and in Poland, buckwheat flour is used to make a dark, crumbly bread with a rich, distinctive flavor. Because buckwheat flour does not contain any gluten, the rising qualities of dough made with it are poor, so it is often mixed with a varying proportion of wheat flour. Buckwheat bread does not slice firmly like ordinary bread so it is baked in flat shapes to be cut into wedges. It is an excellent accompaniment to salads and hearty soups.

MAKES ONE 10-INCH LOAF

1½ cups warm water (105° to 115°F)
2 cakes (0.6 oz.) compressed fresh yeast or 2 packages active-dry yeast
3¾ cups buckwheat flour
1⅓ cups white bread flour
1 teaspoon salt
½ cup (1 stick) butter, melted, plus extra for greasing

Put ⅔ cup of the water into a small bowl. Crumble or sprinkle in the yeast. Leave fresh yeast 5 minutes and dry 15 minutes.

In a large mixing bowl, combine both types of flour and the salt. Make a well in the center and pour in the melted butter. Gradually begin to stir it in. Add the yeast liquid and the remaining water. Mix to a dough and then knead in the bowl until it is smooth. Cover the dough with a clean dish towel and leave in a warm place 1½ hours, or until it doubles in volume.

Knead the dough once again in the bowl. Press it into a greased 10-inch tart pan with a removable bottom. Leave in a warm place 30 minutes to rise. Meanwhile, heat the oven to 350°F. Bake 30 minutes, or until the bread sounds hollow when tapped. Very carefully lift the bread out of the pan, using the removable bottom, and slide it onto a wire rack to cool. It will be very crumbly at this stage, so handle it gently; it will firm up as it cools.

DANISH CRISPBREADS

The crispbread was devised in Scandinavia where summers are short and the wheat harvested early. To save work in the long, hard winters, the wheat was ground immediately and made into breads with a long storage time. Rye is the most widely grown grain in Denmark, so it is the principal flour in the following recipe. Eat the crispbreads simply buttered, or enjoy them with cheeses, dips, pâtés, and salads.

MAKES EIGHT 10-INCH OR SIXTEEN 5-INCH CRISPBREADS

1¼ cups plus 2 tablespoons boiling water
2 tablespoons butter
1¾ cups plus 2 tablespoons whole rye flour
½ cup plus 2 tablespoons whole-wheat flour
¾ cup cake flour
½ teaspoon salt

Heat the oven to 450°F. Pour the water into a large mixing bowl and whisk in the butter. Mix the flours and salt together. Beat them into the water and butter, a little at a time. Use a wooden spoon at first, then knead in the final third of the flour with your hand. Turn the mixture onto a floured work surface and knead until it is smooth.

Divide the dough into 8 or 16 pieces. Roll the large pieces into 10-inch circles and smaller pieces into 5-inch circles. Place the rounds on floured cookie sheets. Bake about 5 minutes, or until crisp but only very lightly colored. Cool them on wire racks. If you have to bake several batches in succession because all the crispbreads will not fit into your oven, cool the cookie sheets completely between batches.

Crispbreads can be stored by wrapping them in fours in a double layer of plastic wrap. Keep them in a cool, dry place.

Pizza and Calzone

The pizza was invented in Naples in the eighteenth century and has spread around the world, providing a complete meal in itself.

A nourishing combination of bread and savory flavorings, a use for tomatoes when they arrived from the New World, an indication of the price of food, and a way to show the colors of the Italian flag—the pizza has been all of these, but essentially it is a complete meal .

Ever since Roman times, the Italians have been fond of small, flat, savory-topped breads. The Romans baked them on heated stones and brushed them with mixtures of olive oil, herbs, and honey. Today, in the region of Romagna, small round breads, enriched with pork fat, are topped with ham, salami, or local cheese and folded in half to make an easily eaten snack.

The pizza, as the rest of the world knows it today, was first devised in Naples in the eighteenth century, and owes its existence to the discovery of tomatoes in the Americas. Tomatoes first arrived in Italy in the late sixteenth century, but it took some time for them to become established as a crop and for new varieties, suited to the Italian climate, to be developed. The area around Naples proved to have the perfect climate for growing tomatoes, and at harvest time they were stewed in large cooking pots to make a rich sauce to serve with meats and add to casseroles. It was very soon discovered the sauce also made an ideal topping for the local flat bread.

Pizzas have rarely been made at home in Italy. When they first appeared, they were sold from stalls in the streets. By the nineteenth century, their fame had spread and *pizzerie* (pizza stores or restaurants) had been set up all over Naples. One such store, the *Pietro il Pizzaiolo*, became so renowned news of it spread to Queen Margherita in Rome. She visited Naples in 1889 and went straight to the store to try its wares. She was given three different pizzas to sample: one was topped simply with tomatoes, garlic and oil; another with pork fat, cheese, and basil; but her favorite was the one with tomatoes, mozzarella cheese, and basil (the colors of the Italian flag). This one became the standard Pizza Napolitana, that is still the most popular pizza today.

Italian immigrants brought the pizza to the United States, where pizzerias were soon set up. The pizza is now available throughout most of the world.

There is an art in making a perfect pizza dough, and many Italian housewives buy either finished pizzas or the dough. The Neapolitan *pizzaioli* are able to stretch the dough so it is almost paper thin before adding the topping.

However, it is not difficult to make a pizza yourself, including the dough, using white bread flour, yeast, and water. Adding a little olive oil gives a crisper edge to the baked crust.

Basic Pizza Dough

Makes one 10-inch pizza or two 7-inch pizzas

1⅔ cups white bread flour
1 cake (0.6 oz.) compressed fresh yeast or 1 package active-dry yeast
⅔ cup warm water (105° to 115°F)
1 teaspoon salt
1 tablespoon olive oil

Make up the dough as for the Basic Loaf dough on page 30, adding the olive oil with the water. Knead it and leave it to rise in the usual way.
For one large pizza, roll the dough into 11-inch circle. Fold over ½ inch all the way around. To make individual pizzas, divide the dough in half and roll each piece to an 8-inch circle.
Place the dough on a cookie sheet and put your chosen filling on top, leaving a border of about ¾ inch. Leave the pizza 20 minutes to rise.
Meanshile, heat the oven to 400°F. Bake 15 minutes, or until the bread is baked through but not too browned around the edges.
If possible, eat the pizza hot so both base and topping are the perfect texture.

Tomato Sauce for Pizza

For one 10-inch or two 7-inch pizzas

1 pound ripe tomatoes
2 tablespoons olive oil
1 small onion, finely chopped (optional)
1 garlic clove, finely chopped (optional)

Scald, skin, and chop the tomatoes. Heat the oil in a skillet over low heat. If you are adding onions and/or garlic, gently soften them in the oil. Add the tomatoes and simmer, stirring frequently, 50 minutes, or until a thick purée forms. Leave the purée to cool before spooning it over the pizza.

Pizza Napolitana

Basic Pizza Dough (left)
Tomato Sauce (above)
6 ounces mozzarella cheese, thinly sliced
1 teaspoon chopped fresh basil or about 15 whole oregano leaves

Spread the tomato sauce over the pizza crust. Place the slices of mozzarella over the tomato sauce and scatter the herbs over the top. Follow the directions under the Basic Pizza Dough recipe for baking.

Calzone

Take some pizza dough, make it into a pocket, fill it with something tasty, and deep-fry it so it is crisp and golden, and you have a *calzone*.

To make *calzone*, use the Basic Pizza Dough and divide it into 2 pieces. Roll each piece into a thin, 8-inch circle. Place your chosen filling ingredients on half the circle. Fold over the other half and seal the edges.

Put about 1½ inches olive or sunflower oil into a saucepan or casserole that will easily hold the *calzone* lying flat; an oval-shaped one is ideal. Heat the oil over high heat. (Olive oil has a relatively low flash point, so take care if using this.)

Put in the first *calzone* and fry it until the underside is golden brown, about 1½ minutes. Turn it over and brown the other side. Lift out the *calzone* with a slotted spoon or pancake turner and put it into a shallow dish lined with paper towels. Fry the others in the same way and serve them as soon as possible.

Fillings for Calzone

Use mozzarella cheese; thin slices of prosciutto or salami; a mixture of ricotta, mozzarella, and pecorino cheeses; or a combination of mozzarella and ham or salami. You can also spread the whole of the top of the dough with ricotta cheese before adding the other filling ingredients.

CHAPATIS

Chapatis have become familiar to the West through Indian restaurants. They are the traditional bread of India, made with a very fine whole-wheat flour and cooked at home on a cast-iron griddle called a *tava*. Chapati flour is sold in Asian food stores and some health-food stores. If it is unavailable, use a half-and-half mixture of white cake flour and whole-wheat flour. Chapatis are simple to make, but the longer the dough is left to stand after mixing, the softer and more pliable the bread will be. Serve the chapatis with curry dishes. In India, they are used as an edible form of eating utensil, small pieces are torn off and wrapped around mouthfuls of food. Brush the loaves repeatedly with water as they bake.

MAKES 8 CHAPATIS

1¾ cups plus 2 tablespoons chapati flour	*1 teaspoon salt*
	up to scant 1 cup water

Put the flour and salt into a bowl. Make a well in the center and gradually stir in ⅔ cup of the water. You need to make a smooth and elastic dough in which the flour has absorbed all the water, so check the consistency and add more water, no more than 1 tablespoon at a time, if necessary. Turn the dough onto a floured work surface and knead 5 to 10 minutes. Wrap it in a wet cloth and leave in a cool place 1 to 2 hours. Alternatively, refrigerate up to 7 hours.

When you are ready to cook, divide the dough into 8 equal-size pieces. Roll each piece into a thin circle about 10 inches in diameter. Once rolled, leave them separate to prevent them from sticking together.

Heat an ungreased griddle over medium heat. Warm a dish in a low oven and a clean, dry dish towel over a radiator or on the side of the stove. Place one chapati on the griddle and cook until it begins to bubble. Turn the chapati over and leave until it is cooked through; for even cooking, turn it several times. Put the cloth in the heated dish and place the first chapati on it. Fold the cloth over it and keep it warm. Cook the remaining chapatis in the same way; make a pile of them as they are ready. Eat them as soon as possible.

NAN

Nan, or naan, bread is eaten in all areas of India, Pakistan, Bangladesh, and Afghanistan, and there are many different types which vary according to the leavening agent used and whether they are plain or made with flavored toppings. In most recipes, the liquid in the dough comes from yogurt. Nan is also made in a variety of sizes. These are large, like the ones you find in Afghanistan. They are soft, with a bouncy texture, and full of flavor.

MAKES THREE 10-INCH OVAL BREADS	ALTERNATIVE TOPPINGS (THESE
3⅓ cups white bread flour	AMOUNTS WILL TOP 8 BREADS)
½ teaspoon salt	*2 tablespoons sesame seeds*
1 cup plus 2 tablespoons plain yogurt	*1 onion, finely chopped*
	2 garlic cloves, crushed
2 cakes (0.6 oz.) compressed fresh yeast or 2 packages active-dry yeast	*4 tablespoons fresh cilantro leaves*
2 eggs, beaten	
6 tablespoons ghee or melted clarified butter	

Put the flour and salt into a bowl and make a well in the center. Gently warm the yogurt to 105° to 115°F and crumble or sprinkle in the yeast. Leave fresh yeast 5 minutes and dry yeast 15 minutes.

Pour the yogurt and yeast liquid into the flour. Add the eggs and 2 tablespoons of the melted *ghee*. Mix to a dough. Turn onto a floured board and knead until it is smooth. Return the dough to the bowl. Cover with a clean dish towel and leave in a warm place 2 hours to rise. It will double in size after 1 hour, but the long rising time gives a distinctive flavor.

Heat the oven to 400°F. Spread aluminum foil over 2 or 3 cookie sheets and heat the cookie sheets and foil in the oven. Prepare your chosen toppings, if using any: leave the sesame seeds and chopped onion as they are; mix the crushed garlic on its own or with the cilantro leaves with the remaining melted *ghee*.

Knead the dough again and divide it into 3 equal pieces. Roll each piece into a 10-inch oval shape, wider at one end than the other. Place the breads on a floured work surface for 10 minutes to rise.

Place the breads on the hot cookie sheets. Either brush them thickly with *ghee* or add one of the toppings; sprinkle the sesame seeds or chopped onion over, or brush them with the *ghee* into which the garlic and cilantro has been mixed.

Bake 7 minutes, or until they are just browned, lightly risen, and still soft. Lift them onto clean towels to cool slightly and serve them warm.

GIRDLE SCONES

"Girdle" is another term for a griddle, or a thick, round cast-iron plate. The term originates from the northern counties of England where this method of cooking breads has remained despite changes to oven cooking. These are best served hot, straight from the griddle, split and buttered, sandwiched back together and cut into wedges. Plain, the scones can be served with sweet or savory spreads or, if currants are added, served with jam or preserves.

MAKES TWO 5-INCH SCONES

2¼ cups plus 2 tablespoons cake
   flour
1 teaspoon salt
½ teaspoon baking soda
6 tablespoons butter, cut into
   pieces, plus extra for
   greasing

1 cup dried currants (optional)
2½ cups sour cream
up to 7 tablespoons milk

Put the flour into a mixing bowl. Add the salt and baking soda and cut in the butter. Stir in the currants, if using. Make a well in the center and pour in all the sour cream. Mix in enough milk to make a smooth, pliable dough.

   Divide the dough in half. Roll each piece into 5-inch circle about ¾ inch thick.

   Heat a lightly greased griddle over low heat. Place one of the dough circles on the griddle and cook 5 to 7 minutes, or until golden brown and firm on one side. Using two pancake turners or metal spatulas, carefully turn over and brown the other side. When done, the scone should sound hollow when tapped.

   Lift the scone onto a wire rack and cool 5 minutes before splitting and buttering it. Cook the other scone in the same way.

KNACKEBROD

Knackebrod are like semisweet oatcakes. In Sweden, where these are the most popular type of crispbread, they are made with a special "hob-nail" rolling pin to make a pattern in the dough as it is rolled. These are equally successful, however, rolled out with a normal rolling pin. Serve with cheeses, dips, and pâtés.

MAKES ABOUT 64 SMALL CRISPBREADS

4 tablespoons shortening
2 tablespoons butter, softened
⅓ cup sugar
1½ cups oatmeal
1¼ cups white bread flour
1 teaspoon salt

1 teaspoon baking soda
¾ cup cultured buttermilk (or
   milk in which you have
   dissolved ½ teaspoon cream
   of tartar)

Cream together the shortening, butter, and sugar in a large mixing bowl. Stir together the oatmeal, flour, salt, and baking soda. Alternately add the flour mixture and the buttermilk to the fats and sugar, working with your hand toward the end to make a stiff dough. With the dough still in the bowl, form it into a ball; put it into the refrigerator 30 minutes.

   Meanwhile, heat the oven to 325°F. Divide the dough into 4 pieces and refrigerate 3 of them. Place the remaining ball of dough on a floured cookie sheet and roll out into a 12-inch square. Prick it all over with a fork. Using a pastry wheel or knife, score the large square into 16 small squares. Do the same with the other pieces of dough.

   Bake the crispbreads 15 to 20 minutes, or until they are crisp and golden. Cool them 2 minutes on the cookie sheets. Transfer to wire racks to cool. Store the crispbreads in an airtight container.

Kachoris and Puris

The Indian city of Benares, in Uttar Pradesh, is one of the holiest cities for the Hindu people. Through it flows the sacred Ganges, and pilgrims come from all over the country to visit, particularly during Diwali, the Festival of Lights.

Many of these pilgrims make their way to Kachori Gulley, the Lane of Fried Breads. Here they buy freshly cooked, small rounds of bread, fried until they are soft in the middle and golden and crisp on the outside. It is said in the city it takes many years to perfect the art of making the perfect kachori. *They should be so light that if 25 are stacked on a plate and you dropped a coin on top, you should still hear the sound of the coin hitting the plate.*

When a kachori is stuffed with a savory filling, it becomes a substantial snack called a puri. *Stuffings include spiced chick-peas or lentils, fenugreek leaves, potatoes stewed with ginger and cumin, and a spiced combination of potatoes and pumpkin. Many Hindus are vegetarians and these foods make a nutritious contribution to their diets.*

87

TORTILLAS

Tortillas are prepared by hand in homes all over Mexico, and there are also tortilla factories and tortilla stores selling them both part-prepared and fully cooked. They are Mexico's national bread, and the name comes from the Spanish word for "little cakes." In Mexico, tortillas are made from *masa*, a paste produced by soaking corn kernels in a solution of lime before grinding them while still wet. *Masa* can be bought fresh in Mexico and the United States. Specialist food stores also sell a flour called *masa harina* or dried *masa*. Like chapatis, tortillas are both food and eating utensils.

MAKES 12 TORTILLAS

2 cups masa harina   *1¼ cups warm water*

Put the *masa harina* into a bowl. Add the water, a little at a time, and gradually mix it into the flour with your hand to make a dough moist enough to roll without pieces crumbling away. Form the dough into a ball and cover it with a clean dish towel. Leave at room temperature 30 minutes.

Divide the dough into 12 equal-size pieces. Place one piece of dough on your left palm and begin to pat it with your right. Turn it around a little and pat it from hand to hand, gently pushing the edge over your palm to spread the dough into a 6-inch circle—this is the traditional Mexican way. Alternatively, if you can't get the knack, roll out the balls of dough between 2 pieces of plastic wrap.

Heat an ungreased griddle over low heat. Warm a large plate or dish in medium oven with a clean, dry dish towel. Place a tortilla on the griddle and cook about 1 minute on each side, or until it is cooked through and both sides look dry, speckled, and brown. Place the warmed dish towel on the plate. Put the tortilla onto it and cover with the sides of the cloth. Cook the others in the same way, and make a pile as they are cooked. Serve the tortillas warm.

PITA BREAD

In the Middle East, the word for bread is *khubz*, and what has become known as pita bread in the West is *khubz Arabi* or Arabian bread. In Armenia it is called *pideh* (from where the word pita comes), and is made with whole-wheat flour. The pita, or pitta, is probably the most popular bread in the Middle East and it was being made in Babylon and Assyria in Biblical times. Pita bread is made from the Basic Bread Dough (see page 30). It is the cooking method that produces the characteristic "pocket." An opened pita bread makes a convenient container for many types of Middle Eastern food.

MAKES 10 PITA BREADS

*Basic Loaf Dough made with   whole-wheat bread flour, or
3⅓ cups white bread flour   a mixture of both*

Make the dough in the usual way (page 30) and leave it in a warm place 1 hour to rise.

Knead the dough for the second time and divide it into 10 pieces. Roll each piece into an 8- x 5-inch oval. Place the pieces on a floured work surface and cover them with a clean dish towel. Leave them 20 minutes to rise. Meanwhile, heat the oven to 450°F.

Flour as many cookie sheets as you will need to take all the breads, and put them into the oven for 5 minutes to become hot; putting the breads on hot cookie sheets in a hot oven bakes them on both sides at once, and will make the pockets form. Place the breads on the hot cookie sheets and put them into the oven 15 minutes, or until they are only just beginning to brown.

Wrap the breads in a clean dish towel to cool slightly, then eat them warm. Alternatively, let them cool completely and reheat them under a broiler when ready to serve.

PARATHAS

Parathas are more substantial than chapatis because they are slightly thicker and made with milk and *ghee*, an Indian fat similar to melted clarified butter. (Look for it in cans in Asian food stores.) A vegetable *ghee* can also be used. *Parathas* are eaten alongside curry dishes, rather than being used to wrap around mouthfuls of food.

MAKES 6 PARATHAS

1¾ cups plus 2 tablespoons chapati flour	*7 tablespoons water*
½ teaspoon salt	*7 tablespoons milk*
1 teaspoon cumin seeds, optional	*½ cup ghee or clarified butter, melted*

Put the flour, salt, and cumin seeds into a bowl. Mix together the water and milk. Stir them into the flour, a little at a time, to make a soft, pliable dough. Turn the dough onto a floured work surface and knead 5 minutes. Wrap it in a wet dish towel and leave it in a cool place 1 to 2 hours, or in the refrigerator up to 7 hours.

When you are ready to cook, divide the dough into 6 equal pieces. Roll each one into a flat 6-inch circle. Brush the top surface with melted *ghee*. Gather up the sides of the circle of dough and twist them together in the center to form a pouch shape. Turn the dough over, twisted side down, and roll out to a diameter of about 7 inches. Leave the rounds separate as they are prepared.

Warm a dish in a warm oven and a dish towel over a radiator or on the stovetop. Heat a griddle over medium heat and brush it with *ghee*. Place a *paratha* on the griddle and cook until the top begins to look as if it is drying, about 2 minutes. Brush with a little *ghee* and cook until the underside is speckled brown, 1 minute longer. Turn over and cook it until the second side is speckled and cooked through.

Put the cloth in the heated dish and place the first *paratha* on it. Fold the cloth over it; keep it warm. Cook the remaining *parathas* in the same way, making a pile as they are cooked. Eat them as soon as possible.

Spiced Parathas

Divide the *ghee* or clarified butter into 2 portions, one for the initial brushing when the *parathas* are rolled, and the other for cooking. Use the cumin seeds in the recipe above. Add ½ teaspoon ground turmeric and ½ teaspoon ground coriander to the *ghee* for brushing. The spices can be varied according to taste. For example, replace the turmeric and coriander with 1 teaspoon *garam masala* and a pinch cayenne pepper.
Cook as above.

Stuffed Parathas

Parathas can be stuffed with spiced, cooked mixtures of vegetables, lentils, or meat. The most popular filling is made from grated raw mooli, or white radish. Grate about 3 ounces white radish and mix it with 1 finely chopped fresh green chili, ½ teaspoon ground ginger, and ½ teaspoon ground coriander. Leave the mixture to stand 1 hour before using. To stuff *parathas* with any chosen mixture, put 1 to 2 teaspoons of the stuffing into the center of the circle of dough after the first rolling. Bring the edges of the dough up around the filling and make the pouch shape as above. Turn over and roll out as for plain *parathas*, so the stuffing is spread inside the dough.
Cook as above.

FOCACCIA

Focaccia is a soft Italian flat bread, about 1 inch thick, traditionally baked in large, round copper baking pans in a brick oven. In its simplest form, it is either baked plain or topped with a liberal sprinkling of salt and several tablespoons olive oil, but there are many regional variations, both savory and sweet. Focaccia is a favorite outdoor food, popular for both barbecues and picnics, and it is also served with cheese and with first courses.

MAKES ONE 10-INCH LOAF

1 cup plus 2 tablespoons warm water (105° to 115°F)

1 cake (0.6 oz.) compressed fresh yeast or 1 package active-dry yeast

scant 3 cups white bread flour

3 tablespoons olive oil

2 teaspoons salt

TOPPING

3 tablespoons olive oil

1 teaspoon salt

4 fresh sage leaves, finely chopped

Put the water into a large mixing bowl. Crumble or sprinkle in the yeast. Leave fresh yeast 5 minutes and dry 15 minutes.

Stir in the flour, oil, and salt. Form the mixture into a smooth dough. Turn out onto a floured work surface and knead until smooth. Return the dough to the bowl and cover with a clean dish towel. Leave in a warm place 1 hour, or until it doubles in volume.

Knead the dough again and roll it into a 10-inch circle. Put it into a shallow, 10-inch square baking pan and leave it in a warm place 30 minutes to rise. Meanwhile, heat the oven to 400°F. Dimple the top of the loaf with your fingertips. Spoon the oil evenly over the top and sprinkle with the sage.

Bake 20 to 25 minutes, or until it is golden brown. Transfer to a wire rack to cool.

APPLE *and* WALNUT CRUMBLE CAKE

This is based on a German favorite called *Streuselkuchen*, which means "crumble cake." It is a combination of sliced apples and chopped walnuts sandwiched between a light, sweet, yeasted base and a crunchy crumble topping. It is delicious both served warm as a dessert or sliced at room temperature with morning coffee or afternoon tea.

MAKES ONE 11- X 7-INCH LOAF

4 tablespoons warm water (105° to 115°F)
1 cake (0.6 oz.) compressed fresh yeast or 1 package active-dry yeast
⅔ cup warm milk (105° to 115°F)
grated peel of ½ lemon
5 tablespoons sugar
1 egg
2 egg yolks
2 cups plus 2 tablespoons white bread flour

7 tablespoons butter, cut into small pieces and softened

TOPPING
1 cup plus 2 tablespoons cake flour
1 teaspoon ground cinnamon
10 tablespoons (1¼ sticks) butter, cut into small pieces and softened
6 tablespoons sugar
2 dessert apples
½ cup shelled walnuts, finely chopped

Pour the water into a small mixing bowl. Crumble or sprinkle in the yeast. Leave fresh yeast 5 minutes and dry yeast 15 minutes. Stir in the milk and lemon peel.

In a large mixing bowl, beat together the sugar, egg, and egg yolks. Stir in the yeast and milk mixture. Gradually add the flour and beat with a wooden spoon to make a soft dough. Turn the dough onto a floured work surface and knead until smooth. Return the dough to the bowl. Cover with a clean dish towel and leave 1 hour to rise, or until it doubles in volume. Meanwhile, heat the oven to 375°F. Butter a 17- x 11-inch shallow cake pan.

To make the topping, put the flour into a bowl with half the cinnamon. Cut in 7 tablespoons of the butter and all the sugar. Peel and slice the apples. Melt the remaining butter.

Knead the risen dough and roll it out to fit the pan; place dough in the pan. Arrange a layer of apples over the dough and sprinkle with the walnuts and remaining cinnamon. Cover with the crumble mixture. Sprinkle the melted butter over.

Leave the cake to rest in a warm place 10 minutes. Bake 45 minutes, or until the top is crunchy and the base is baked through. Leave to cool slightly in the pan before cutting into squares. Serve it warm or at room temperature.

CRUMPETS

Crumpets are a well-loved English teatime treat. They are cooked on a griddle, cooled, and then toasted. Because they are made from a liquid batter, crumpets are made in metal crumpet rings; you only need 2 rings because they are slipped off while the crumpets cook. (Look for these from specialist cookware stores.) The inside of homemade crumpets is light and airy and the tops fairly smooth. Once toasted, serve them hot and buttered.

MAKES 8 CRUMPETS

1¼ cups warm milk (105° to 115°F)
1 cake (0.6 oz.) compressed fresh yeast or 1 package active-dry yeast
2 tablespoons butter, softened, plus extra of greasing
1⅔ cups white bread flour
1 teaspoon salt
1 egg, beaten

Put half the milk into a small bowl. Crumble or sprinkle in the yeast. Leave fresh yeast 5 minutes and dry yeast 15 minutes. Melt the butter in the remaining milk.

Put the flour and salt into a large mixing bowl and make a well in the center. Using a wooden spoon, beat in the yeast liquid, the milk and butter mixture and the egg to make a thick batter. Cover with a dish towel and leave in a warm place 1 hour, or until light and bubbly.

Grease a cast-iron griddle and warm it over low heat. Lightly grease the crumpet rings and put them on the griddle. Spoon 2 tablespoons batter into each ring. Cook about 3 minutes until the sides are firm and the underside firm and browned. Using a metal spatula, slip the rings off the crumpets; do not touch the rings with your bare hands—they will be hot! Turn the crumpets over and cook the second side. Start another 2 crumpets alongside the first, using the same rings, cleaned if necessary. Re-grease the griddle if it becomes dry.

When the first 2 crumpets are done, lift them onto a wire rack to cool. To serve, toast the crumpets on each side under a broiler so the outsides become firm and dry, then butter them.

Injera

What the chapati is to Indian meals, and the tortilla to Mexican, the injera *is to Ethiopian cooking.*

Injera *are larger than either chapatis or tortillas, about 17 inches across, round, and very thin. They are made of* teff *flour, ground from the finest and most delicate member of the millet family.*

Teff *flour and water are combined to make enough batter for about 30 flat breads, and then left to ferment for 3 to 4 days.* Injera *are cooked on a large, ceramic griddle, heated over a wood fire. The first batch of batter is poured in a spiral fashion, starting from the outside. Unlike most flat breads, the* injera *is covered while it is cooking with a domed lid sealed at the edges with a damp rag. Each* injera *is cooked individually, taking only a few minutes. Most families make enough to last them several days.*

Because of the long fermenting time, injera *have a slightly sour flavor. They are often used as both utensil and accompaniment when eaten with a spicy stew called a* wat.

CHAPTER FOUR

QUICK BREADS

There are many bread recipes from around the world which require very little time to prepare. Take a break from a busy schedule to refresh and treat yourself with a delicious and nourishing snack. Rewarding and quick to make, astound your friends with these easy-to-create dishes of delight.

QUICK BREADS

When baking powder and baking soda first became commercially available in the nineteenth century, they opened up the way to making light, leavened breads without having to wait for a dough to rise. Previously, a bread-maker had to wait for the starter, or flour and water batter, to ferment; and the rising time was slow as the leavening relied exclusively on yeasts naturally present in the atmosphere. Versatile quick breads can be sweet or savory; they can be cooked on a griddle, baked in the oven, or steamed in a bowl.

Quick breads are made in many parts of the world. Some, such as the round, flat roti from the Caribbean, are plain and intended to be served with savory foods. Soda bread, from Ireland, is another popular quick bread. It is a round, leavened bread, equally good served with cheese or preserves; it can also be flavored with herbs, spices, dried fruits, and savory ingredients, such as bacon. The recipe for Walnut Soda Bread shows just how versatile the basic recipe can be.

This chapter also includes recipes for tea breads from many parts of the world. These are not as rich as a cake but are lighter and sweeter than everyday breads, and can be served plain or buttered to accompany afternoon tea or coffee. Dutch Gingerbread is golden and chewy, West Indian Coconut Bread tastes of the Caribbean, and Dark Speckled Tea Bread is dense with tea-soaked fruit.

Une boulangerie, *Jean Colombes a Bourges 15th century*

MUFFINS

Muffins are made with baking powder and, in shape and texture, are more like cakes than the yeasted, griddle-cooked English muffin. They have been a popular breakfast bread for most of the twentieth century, and many housewives have their own favorite sweet or savory flavoring.

This is the basic recipe. It uses a mixture of two types of flour, but either one can be used alone.

MAKES 10 MUFFINS

1 cup plus 2 tablespoons cake flour
3/4 cup plus 2 tablespoons whole-wheat flour
1 teaspoon salt
2 teaspoons baking powder

2 tablespoons sugar (white or brown, according to taste)
1 cup plus 2 tablespoons milk
1 egg, beaten
3 tablespoons shortening, melted

Heat the oven to 400°F. Arrange 10 muffin paper cupcake cases in a cake pan. Put the flours into a bowl. Stir in the salt, baking powder, and sugar. Make a well in the center. Beat in the milk, egg, and shortening to make a thick batter. Half fill the paper cases with the batter. Bake 20 minutes, or until the muffins are risen and baked through. Transfer to a wire rack to cool.

Prayer

"That he may bring food out of the earth, and wine that maketh the heart of man: and oil to make him a cheerful countenance, and bread to strengthen man's heart."

PRAYER BOOK

POTATO SCONES

Potato scones are a traditional English teatime treat from Lancashire. They are also popular in parts of the United States and Canada. Potato scones can be cooked on a griddle for a soft texture or on a cookie sheet in the oven for a firm finish. Serve the scones warm and buttered, with preserves or with cheese, or use them to accompany a cooked dish such as a casserole or stew. Any leftovers can be split and toasted and enjoyed with a cup of tea.

MAKES ABOUT 15 SCONES

10 ounces potatoes
4 tablespoons butter, cut into small pieces and softened
4 tablespoons whole milk
approximately 1 1/4 cups cake flour or whole-wheat flour

1/4 teaspoon salt
1/2 teaspoon baking soda

Boil the potatoes in their skins until they are tender; this gives the scones a better flavor and texture. Drain them and peel them while they are still warm, and push them through a strainer into a mixing bowl. Beat in the butter and milk until thoroughly incorporated.

Mix the flour with the salt and baking soda. Using a wooden spoon at first and then your hand, gradually work the flour into the potatoes to make a manageable dough. Potatoes vary in texture; if the dough is very stiff before all the flour is added, you may not need all of it. If your dough is still quite moist after incorporating all the flour, you may need to add a very little more, 1 tablespoon at a time.

Turn the dough onto a floured work surface and roll out to a thickness of about 1/2 inch. Using a 2 1/2-inch biscuit cutter, stamp out 15 scones. Leave the scones to rest in a warm place 15 minutes. Either heat an oven to 400°F or lightly grease a griddle.

If you are using the oven, place the scones on a lightly floured cookie sheet and bake 15 minutes, or until golden brown. If you are using the griddle, heat it over low heat. Cook the scones on the griddle about 7 minutes on each side, or until they are golden brown and cooked through.

99

ORANGE *and* APRICOT TEA BREAD

Fruity tea breads made with whole-wheat flour are popular in Australia and New Zealand. In the following recipe, dried apricots are used to give texture and flavor, and also to act as a sugar substitute. Using a microwave and a food processor will speed up the soaking and mixing times considerably, but they are not necessary.

MAKES ONE LOAF

1½ cups whole dried apricots	*2 cups whole-wheat flour*
1¼ cups pure orange juice	*1 teaspoon baking powder*
1 egg	*¼ teaspoon baking soda*
4 tablespoons sunflower oil	*grated peel of 1 orange*
7 tablespoons milk	

Soak the apricots in the orange juice overnight. Alternatively, put the apricots and orange juice into a bowl and microwave them on Full Power 2 minutes. Leave them to soak 10 minutes longer.

Heat the oven to 350°F. Drain the apricots, reserving the juice; chop half of them. Put the rest into a food processor with ½ cup of the reserved juice, and work into a purée. Add the egg, sunflower oil, and milk and process again until smooth and thick. Add the flour, baking powder, baking soda, and orange peel, and process to make a smooth batter. Add the chopped apricots and process in one or two quick bursts, to keep the apricots in pieces.

(If you are not using a food processor, purée half the apricots in a blender. Put the flour into a bowl and add the baking powder, baking soda, and orange peel. Make a well in the center and add the puréed apricots, egg, and sunflower oil. Begin to beat in flour from the sides of the well and gradually beat in the milk to make a smooth batter. Fold in the chopped apricots.)

Put the mixture into a greased 9- x 5- x 2½-inch bread pan. Bake 40 minutes or until the top of the loaf is brown and a skewer inserted in the center comes out clean. Turn out the loaf onto a wire rack to cool.

GOLDEN SYRUP TEA BREAD

This golden-colored loaf is light and moist. Serve it sliced, plain or buttered, as a midmorning snack or with afternoon tea. Because it is sweet but not sticky, it also makes excellent lunchbox fare. (Look for golden syrup, in its distinctive green and gold cans, in general food stores.)

MAKES ONE LOAF

2⅓ cups cake flour	*1 egg, beaten*
½ teaspoon baking soda	*⅔ cup milk*
¼ nutmeg, grated	*¾ cup raisins*
4 tablespoons light brown sugar	
4 tablespoons golden syrup or honey	

Heat the oven to 350°F. Grease a 9- x 5- x 2½-inch bread pan. Put the flour into a bowl. Stir in the baking soda and the nutmeg. Make a well in the center.

Put the sugar and golden syrup or honey into a saucepan and melt together over low heat. Pour into the well in the flour. Add the egg and milk and gradually beat together to make a thick, smooth batter. Fold in the raisins.

Spoon the batter into the prepared pan. Bake 50 minutes, or until the top is golden brown and a skewer inserted in the center comes out clean. Turn out the loaf onto a wire rack to cool.

DUTCH GINGERBREAD

The Dutch have a sweet tooth, and Dutch Gingerbread has a firm, brown outer crust, and a golden, spicy, very sweet, springy crumb. In the 1930s Countess Morphy described it as "one of the great national Dutch cakes or 'sweet' breads." Serve it plain or buttered.

MAKES ONE LARGE LOAF

4⅓ cups cake flour	*1 teaspoon anise seeds*
3 tablespoons baking powder	*½ teaspoon ground nutmeg*
7 tablespoons dark brown sugar	*1⅔ cups golden syrup*
1 teaspoon ground ginger	*⅔ cup milk*
1 teaspoon ground cinnamon	

Heat the oven to 325°F. Grease a 9- x 5- x 2½-inch bread pan. Put the flour into a bowl. Add the baking powder, sugar, and spices, mixing them together with your fingers.

Make a well in the center and add the golden syrup. Using a wooden spoon, begin to beat the syrup into the flour. Using the wooden spoon at first and then your hand, mix in the milk, a little at a time, until the batter has a soft, dropping consistency.

Spoon the batter into the prepared pan and smooth the top. Bake 1 hour, or until the top is golden brown and a skewer inserted in the center comes out clean. Turn out the loaf onto a wire rack to cool.

Through the Looking-Glass

"A loaf of bread," the Walrus said,
"Is what we chiefly need:
Pepper and vinegar besides
Are very good indeed —
Now if you're ready, Oysters dear,
We can begin to feed."

LEWIS CARROLL, 1832–1898

Corn Breads

Corn bread is made from cornmeal and features widely in country and frontier recipes. It is delicious with stews, bean dishes, or soup, or can be eaten on its own with butter or jam.

Toward the end of the fifteenth century, the Spaniards and the Portuguese discovered, in what is now Cuba, small fields of a tall, waving plant which the locals called by a name that sounded like "may-ees." Since then, this crop has become a staple in many parts of the world.

Maize, as the Europeans first termed it, yielded large husks of pea-size grains, which formed the staple diet of the islanders. The yields were large, far larger than from the same area planted with wheat, and the plant was suited to the hot, dry climate. It was the perfect food for both land and people, and the newcomers were quick to realize its worth.

The Europeans also called it "corn," which was their word for all food grains. To distinguish it from the corn at home, it was termed "Indian corn," or "sweetcorn."

Corn is still grown in the West Indies, where it was discovered, and there it is a frequent ingredient in sweet tea breads. It was also taken back to Europe in the sixteenth century. It was unloaded at Rialto in Venice and was soon made into polenta, which is still one of the staple foods of the area. Polenta is a thick, boiled porridge left to set set in a pan. It can

then be eaten immediately or can be baked or deep-fried to give it a golden, crisp outside.

Corn also found its way back to Portugal, and there it is made into a yeasted bread called *broa* with a crumbly texture and strong corn flavor to make it an excellent accompaniment to hearty spiced soups and main dishes.

The Mexicans and the Peruvians had eaten corn for hundreds of years. They had developed it from a small, coarse grass and produced hundreds of varieties for different climates and altitudes, varying in color, size, and ease of cooking. In Mexico the tortilla made from corn was, and in some areas still is, served at every meal.

Seventeenth-century settlers found the crop much farther north in the American heartland, and when their own European wheat crops failed, owing mainly to an unfamiliar climate, they learned from the Native Americans how to grow and how to survive on corn.

The flour produced from corn is coarse and golden yellow. Pioneers pushing back the frontiers of America found it convenient to carry and easy to make into quick-cooking cakes and breads over campfires. The earliest corn breads

Corn pone was once cooked over the campfires of the pioneers.

Corn Pone

Makes 8 small cakes

1½ cups plus 2 tablespoons cornmeal
1 teaspoon salt
1 teaspoon baking soda
2 tablespoons shortening
⅔ cup boiling water
⅔ cup cultured buttermilk (or milk soured with ½ teaspoon cream of tartar)

Heat the oven to 350°F. Put the cornmeal, salt, and baking soda into a mixing bowl. Rub in the shortening. Make a well in the center. Pour in the boiling water, stirring in the cornmeal from the sides of the well. Add enough of the buttermilk to make a soft, pliable dough. Divide the dough into 8 pieces and form each one into a round, flat cake. Put them onto a floured cookie sheet. Bake 20 minutes, or until the edges are brown. Eat them hot and buttered.

It was a hard life on the first wagon trains across America. The pioneers soon learned to adapt to their new environment, making various types of corn bread in the American-Indian fashion.

Cornmeal, sometimes called maize meal, is a coarse, yellow flour with a delicious nutty scent.

consisted of cornmeal mixed to a dough or paste with water. Small cakes were cooked over hot ashes in a skillet with legs, called a spider, or in makeshift ovens.

Eventually, the new settlers came to enjoy Indian corn. At first they had to eat it or starve, but even when the vast wheatlands were eventually established, corn was still grown on a large scale. Hundreds of new varieties were developed and the old corn bread recipes were still used when traveling had ceased and new houses were built. Corn bread now epitomizes American country cooking.

One of the simplest corn breads is corn pone. The name came originally from the Indian *apone*, meaning cakes made with cornmeal and water that were cooked in the ashes. These were quickly copied by the settlers and called pone, or ash cakes. They were cooked either on a spider or on a hoe held over the flames, when they were called hoe cakes. The recipe on the left comes from the early nineteenth century, when baking soda became available as a leavening agent.

Johnny Cake was another corn bread made by pioneers. A variety of ingredients, such as sugar or molasses, can be added, and the amount of milk or water used varies with different recipes, but the bread is always baked in a flat pan, either in the oven, in a spider, or on a griddle. The name may come from

Johnny Cake with Molasses

Makes one 10- x 8-inch cake

1 cup plus 2 tablespoons cornmeal
1⅓ cups all-purpose flour
2 teaspoons baking powder
1 teaspoon salt
1 tablespoon molasses
6 tablespoons shortening
2 cups milk, or half milk and half water

Heat the oven to 350°F. Put the cornmeal, flour, baking powder, and salt into a mixing bowl. Rub in the molasses and shortening. Make a well in the center. Gradually beat in the milk to make a thick batter. Pour the batter into a greased 10- x 8-inch baking pan. Bake 30 minutes, or until the cake is golden brown on top and a skewer inserted into the center comes out clean. Turn out onto a wire rack and eat it hot.

"journey cake," meaning it was cooked by the side of the western trail. Or it may be a corruption of the name of the Shawnee Indian tribe who may have been responsible for teaching the early settlers how to make corn bread. No one really knows. Johnny Cakes should be eaten hot and buttered. They make an excellent accompaniment to savory stews, bean dishes, and soups, but is equally good simply spread with jam.

ROTI

Roti is a Caribbean flat bread, descended from the chapatis and *puris* that were first introduced to the area by settlers from the Indian continent. *Rotis* are large and thin, baked quickly on a griddle, and traditionally served with curries. For the local carnival in Port of Spain, Trinidad, the Indian population prepares enormous mounds of *rotis* and fills them to order with a selection of curries and spiced meats and legumes. Like so many of the flat breads, *rotis* act as both food and food holder.

MAKES 4 ROTIS

2 cups cake flour	*⅔ cup cold water*
1 teaspoon baking powder	*6 tablespoons ghee, melted*
1 teaspoon salt	*(unsalted butter may be used*
3 tablespoons butter	*instead)*

Put the flour into a bowl. Stir in the baking powder and salt. Cut in the butter. Make a well in the center. Pour in the water and mix to a soft, pliable dough. Turn the dough onto a floured work surface and knead until it is smooth. Return it to the bowl, cover with a clean dish towel and let rest in a warm place 30 minutes.

Knead the dough again and divide it into 4 equal pieces. Roll each piece into a 10-inch circle. Fold the circle in half and then half again. Roll the folded pieces of dough into circles again, shaping the circles using your hands and the rolling pin.

Heat an ungreased griddle over medium heat. Warm a dish in a low oven and have ready a clean, dry dish towel. Place one *roti* on the griddle and cook about 1 minute until dry but not colored on the underside. Turn it over and brush the top with melted *ghee*. Cook 2 minutes longer, then brush on more *ghee* and continue to cook 1 minute; the top should be bubbling and sizzling. Turn the *roti* over again and finish cooking the first side about 2 minutes, or until it is brown and crisp; the *roti* should be cooked through but still pliable. If it is too crisp, place it on a board and bang it with a rolling pin or wooden mallet to break up and flake the outside.

Place the cloth in the heated dish and place the first *roti* on it. Fold the cloth over it to keep it warm. Cook the remaining *rotis* in the same way, adding them to the dish as they are ready.

WEST INDIAN COCONUT BREAD

Sweet breads, leavened with baking soda, are popular in the West Indies. There bakers make the most of a mixture of flours, using wheat flour, corn, tapioca, breadfruit, and banana flours. Local ingredients such as limes and coconuts are also included in these breads. The recipe below makes a moist loaf, with a rich coconut flavor. Serve it sliced, with tea or coffee.

MAKES ONE LARGE LOAF

1 small coconut	*½ teaspoon salt*
1½ cups cake flour	*½ cup plus 2 tablespoons sugar*
½ cup cornmeal	*½ cup (1 stick) unsalted butter,*
2 teaspoons baking powder	*melted*
½ teaspoon ground cinnamon	*7 tablespoons evaporated milk*
½ teaspoon ground nutmeg	*3 tablespoons raisins*
½ teaspoon ground cloves	*3 tablespoons golden raisins*
grated peel of 1 lime	

Heat the oven to 350°F. Grease a 9- x 5- x 2½-inch bread pan. Use a skewer to pierce through the two "eyes" of the coconut. Pour the liquid from the inside into a measuring jug; reserve 3 ounces coconut water. Using a heavy hammer, break open the coconut. Remove the white flesh and, using a potato peeler, peel away the brown rind. Grate the flesh, either by hand or using a food processor.

Put the flours and baking powder into a bowl. Add the spices, lime peel, salt, and sugar and mix together. Stir in the grated coconut. Make a well in the center and add the butter. Gradually beat in the coconut water and the evaporated milk until the batter has a soft, dropping consistency. Fold in the raisins and golden raisins.

Put the batter into the prepared pan. Bake 40 minutes, or until the loaf is golden brown and a skewer inserted in the center comes out clean. Turn out the loaf onto a wire rack to cool.

STEAMED BROWN BREAD

Steamed bread, made with a mixture of flours, is said to have originated around Boston, and also along the St. Lawrence River in Canada. There is an Australian version as well, cooked in a billycan, called Brown Billy Loaf. This recipe contains cornmeal, white cake flour, and whole-wheat flour. For a fuller flavor, substitute rye flour for the white.

Steamed brown bread is quick to mix but has a very long cooking time.

This bread is traditionally served hot with baked beans, but it can also be cooled, sliced, buttered, and eaten like ordinary bread.

MAKES ONE LOAF

½ cup cornmeal
½ cup cake flour
scant ½ cup whole-wheat flour
½ teaspoon salt
½ teaspoon baking soda
2 tablespoons molasses

1 cup plus 2 tablespoons
  cultured buttermilk, plain
  yogurt, or plain milk in
  which you have dissolved 1
  teaspoon cream of tartar
⅓ cup raisins (optional)

Put all the flours into a bowl. Stir in the salt and baking soda. Make a well in the center and add the molasses. Gradually stir in the liquid to make a thick batter. Stir in the raisins, if using.

Pour the batter into a greased 2½-cup heatproof bowl. Cover the bowl with a circle of waxed paper and then a circle of foil, both about 2 inches larger than the top of the bowl. Secure them with string, making a handle with a couple of loops for easy lifting.

Bring a large pan of water to a boil and place a trivet in the bottom. Lower the bowl onto the trivet. Cover the pan and boil the bread 3 hours, topping up the water, with boiling water from a kettle, when necessary; do not let the pan boil dry.

Lift out the bowl and turn out the bread. Serve it sliced hot with baked beans or a spicy casserole, or cooled, sliced, and buttered.

Della Lutes

Della Lutes was brought up in a farmhouse in southern Michigan in the 1880s and 1890s. In 1938, in England, she published a book about her memories called The Country Kitchen. *It is about 'Lijer and 'Miry, her father and mother, and their farmworkers, Adelaide and Big Jim. It is written through the eyes of a child who watched with fascination the growing, harvesting, and preparation of food. The center of her world was the farmhouse kitchen, where, among other things, she helped her mother bake bread:*

"In the days when men wrested an entire living from the soil, there was little talk about dieting, and little need of it... They ate strong food, and bread was believed to be the staff of life...

"We ate meat and potatoes and pancakes. We drank quantities of milk, ate acres of bread, consumed butter by the pound, and we also ate doughnuts and cookies by the dozen. My pleasantest memory is of breakfast in a nice warm kitchen on a cold morning, with my little glass mug of milk, a huge slice of bread all buttered at once, some little pancakes cooked just for me, and my eye on the cookie plate."

For the New Year celebrations, "the breads were given a fair start the previous evening and then baked on the morning before the arrival of the guests. Yeast bread, salt-risin' bread, and 'riz' biscuits, filling the large, sunny old kitchen with a warm, crusty fragrance which, mingled with that of roasting meat and spices released from fruity jars, teased the appetite almost beyond endurance."

107

DARK SPECKLED TEA BREAD

Dark tea breads, densely speckled with dried fruits, are popular in the British Isles. Make the fruits moist and plump by soaking them in tea. Serve this delicious loaf sliced and generously buttered.

MAKES ONE LARGE LOAF

generous 1 cup raisins	*1 teaspoon apple-pie spice*
generous 1 cup golden raisins	*½ cup (1 stick) butter*
2¼ cups hot black tea	*generous ¼ cup dark brown*
2 cups whole-wheat flour	* sugar*
2⅓ cups cake flour	*1 egg, beaten*
2 teaspoons baking soda	*1 tablespoon molasses*
1 teaspoon salt	*⅔ cup plain yogurt*

Put the raisins and golden raisins into a bowl and pour the tea over. Leave them at least 4 hours. Drain the fruits; reserve the tea.

Heat the oven to 350°F. Grease a 9- x 5- x 2½-inch bread pan. Put both flours into a bowl. Stir in the baking soda, salt, and mixed spice. Cut in the butter. Add the sugar and stir in the drained fruits. Make a well in the center. Add the egg and molasses or treacle. Gradually beat the yogurt and ⅔ cup of the reserved tea into the flour to make a stiff batter.

Put the batter into the prepared pan. Bake 40 minutes, or until a skewer inserted in the center comes out clean. Turn out the tea bread onto a wire rack to cool.

WALNUT SODA BREAD

This is an example of how to enrich and flavor plain soda bread. Serve either plain or buttered.

MAKES ONE LOAF

1¾ cups plus 2 tablespoons whole-wheat flour
½ teaspoon baking soda
1 teaspoon salt
3 tablespoons butter
2 tablespoons chopped fresh parsley
1 tablespoon chopped fresh thyme

⅓ cup shelled walnuts, finely chopped
1 onion, finely chopped
⅔ cup cultured buttermilk, plain yogurt, or plain milk in which you have dissolved ½ teaspoon cream of tartar

Heat the oven to 400°F. Put the flour into a mixing bowl. Stir in the baking soda and salt. Cut in 2 tablespoons butter. Add the herbs and walnuts. Soften the onion in the remaining butter in a small skillet over low heat. Add to the flour mixture.

Make a well in the center of the flour. Pour in the liquid and mix to form a dough. Turn it onto a floured board and knead lightly. Roll it into a circle about 1 inch thick. Place the circle on a floured cookie sheet and score the top into 8 sections.

Bake 20 minutes, or until the top is lightly browned. Transfer to a wire rack and eat warm or at room temperature.

SODA BREAD

Soda bread is popular in many countries of the world, but nowhere more so than in Ireland, where both brown and white varieties fill the bakeries. It is easy to make and you can vary the ingredients according to availability. Soda bread is equally good with cheese and savories, as well as with sweet preserves. It is also excellent plain and buttered.

MAKES ONE LOAF

1¼ cups plus 2 tablespoons flour, either whole-wheat, white cake flour, or a mixture—proportions according to taste
½ teaspoon salt
½ teaspoon baking soda

2 tablespoons butter
⅔ cup cultured buttermilk, plain yogurt, or plain milk in which you have dissolved ½ teaspoon cream of tartar

Heat the oven to 400°F. Put the flour into a bowl. Stir in the salt and baking soda. Cut in the butter. Make a well in the center. Pour in the liquid and mix to form a dough. Turn out onto a floured board and knead lightly. Form into a ball and press, or roll into a circle about 1½ inches thick.

Place the dough on a floured cookie sheet and score the top into quarters. Bake 20 minutes, or until just colored and the loaf sounds hollow when tapped on the bottom. Transfer to a wire rack to cool.

Variations

Add any of the following to the flour:

1 teaspoon Italian seasoning or 1 tablespoon chopped fresh herbs

•

½ teaspoon caraway or cumin seeds

•

4 tablespoons grated cheddar cheese

•

1 onion, chopped and softened in oil or butter

CARROT TEA BREAD

Light and moist, the sweetness in this recipe is supplied by the carrots and dried fruits, as well as a small amount of sugar. Without the filling, it makes popular lunchbox fare. The addition of the filling makes it ideal for enjoying with a cup of tea or coffee.

MAKES ONE LOAF

2⅓ cups whole-wheat flour
2 teaspoons baking powder
1 teaspoon ground cinnamon
1 teaspoon ground nutmeg
½ cup light brown sugar
1 large carrot, peeled and grated
2 ounces dried apricots, soaked or "no-soak" apricots

½ cup golden raisins
1 egg
4 tablespoons sunflower oil
½ cup carrot juice
4 tablespoons milk

FILLING (OPTIONAL):
¼ cup fromage blanc
2 teaspoons honey

Heat the oven to 350°F. Grease a 9- x 5- x 2½-inch bread pan. Put the flour into a mixing bowl. Stir in the baking powder, spices, sugar, carrot, and dried fruits. In a separate bowl, beat together the egg, oil, carrot juice, and milk.

Make a well in the center of the flour mixture. Pour in the liquid mixture and gradually beat it into the flour.

Spoon the batter into the prepared pan. Bake 35 minutes, or until the loaf is risen and golden and a skewer inserted in the center comes out clean. Turn out the tea bread onto a wire rack to cool.

To make the filling, stir the fromage blanc in a bowl and beat in the honey. When the tea bread is cool, carefully cut the loaf horizontally in half. Spread the lower half with the filling and replace the top.

Serve the loaf cut into slices.

CHAPTER FIVE

BREAD DISHES

Take a simple loaf and transform it into a complete meal. There are infinite ways to create sweet or savory dishes, or to put an interesting spin on an old and trusted favorite. You will be surprised how versatile bread is—from appetizers to desserts, bread dishes can play an important part in any repertoire.

BREAD DISHES

As well as forming a part of a meal—or even being a meal in itself—bread is one of the most versatile ingredients you can find in the kitchen. With a loaf of bread, you have the basis for many easy-to-make dishes, which are also very economical.

Whether sliced, cubed, or made into crumbs, bread can be used to make quick snacks, warming puddings, exciting picnics, and even ice cream. For an exciting alternative to sandwiches when you go on a picnic, hollow out a loaf and fill it with a smoked mackerel pâté or a succulent mixture of tomatoes, anchovies, and olive oil.

Bread can also be used for easy comfort food. Many of us may fondly remember Bread Pudding from childhood, but it can be enjoyed at any age and is worth rediscovering. French Toast, or "eggy bread," is a comfort favorite, but top it with savory vegetables or a sweet vegetable compote and it becomes a meal for adults, quickly prepared and inexpensive.

This Chapter includes bread dishes from all over the world. From Cadiz, in Spain, for example, fresh crumbs are used to thicken Ajo, a hearty winter soup; from Italy, slices of fresh bread are brushed with olive oil or butter and baked to make crisp Crostini; and from the borders of Italy and Austria come savory dumplings called Knödel.

A simple loaf of bread can be a passport to a wide variety of dishes.

Dos molinos, *Jacob van Ruisdael 1655*

Ajo (Garlic Soup)

Ajo is a bread crumb- and-garlic soup prepared every winter in the region surrounding Cadiz in Spain. Garlic and cayenne pepper are popular ingredients for keeping colds and flu at bay and easing their symptoms. The soup is economical and simple to make, and yet very substantial. The original recipe was made only with water, but chicken stock is suggested here for a better flavor; if you are using a stock cube, however, choose a mild one. The soup is pungent and definitely for garlic lovers!

SERVES 4

7 tablespoons olive oil
5 large garlic cloves, crushed
1¼ cups crumbs from day-old
  white bread
2 teaspoons paprika
¼ teaspoon cayenne pepper, or
  more if preferred

4 cups mild chicken stock or
  water
2 eggs, beaten
6 tablespoons chopped fresh
  parsley

Heat the oil in a large saucepan over low heat. Add the crushed garlic and stir 1 minute. Add the bread crumbs and stir continually 10 to 15 minutes, or until they turn golden. Stir in the paprika and cayenne pepper. Pour in the stock or water and bring it to a boil. Cover and simmer very gently 30 minutes, stirring occasionally.

Remove the pan from the heat and gradually beat in the eggs. Return the soup to the heat and heat gently to thicken the eggs, but do not boil. Stir in the chopped parsley and serve hot.

114

Proverb

"Stolen waters are sweet, and bread eaten in
secret is pleasant."

The Bible

KNÖDEL

Knödel come from the northern region of Alto Adige in Italy. These are light, herb-flavored dumplings which can be served with soup or as a side dish with meat and vegetable dishes. They can be eaten plain or with melted butter and chopped sage leaves spooned over them. The original recipe contains the smoked fat called *speck*, but bacon has been substituted in this version; it can be omitted for vegetarians or if a milder flavor is desired.

Another version of *Knödel*, made in the same region, is made with crumbs from a rye and buckwheat breads and the dumplings are served with sauerkraut (fermented cabbage) and tomato sauce.

SERVES 4

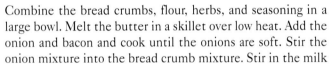

1½ cups bread crumbs from
   day-old white bread
4 tablespoons all-purpose flour
4 tablespoons chopped fresh
   parsley
1 tablespoon chopped
   marjoram
salt and freshly ground black
   pepper
2 tablespoons butter

1 onion, finely chopped
½ cup finely chopped fat bacon
   (optional)
2 eggs, beaten
5 cups chicken or vegetable stock

TOPPING (OPTIONAL)
3 tablespoons butter
5 sage leaves, finely chopped

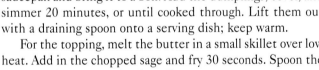

Combine the bread crumbs, flour, herbs, and seasoning in a large bowl. Melt the butter in a skillet over low heat. Add the onion and bacon and cook until the onions are soft. Stir the onion mixture into the bread crumb mixture. Stir in the milk and eggs; leave to stand for 30 minutes.

Form the dough into 8 dumplings. Pour the stock into a saucepan and bring it to a boil. Add the dumplings, cover, and simmer 20 minutes, or until cooked through. Lift them out with a draining spoon onto a serving dish; keep warm.

For the topping, melt the butter in a small skillet over low heat. Add in the chopped sage and fry 30 seconds. Spoon the butter and sage over the dumplings.

BREAD SAUCE

Bread sauce is a traditional English accompaniment to roast meats and game, its mild flavour contrasting well with the richness of the meat. It developed from the medieval custom of serving sweet, bread crumb- or almond-based puddings alongside the meat course.

SERVES 4

1 small onion
4 cloves
1¼ cups milk
½ bay leaf

1 cup fresh white bread crumbs
salt and pepper
2 tablespoons butter, cut into
   small pieces and softened

Peel the onion and stick the cloves into it. Put the milk into a saucepan and bring to a boil; do not let it boil over. Add the onion and the bay leaf. Cover the pan, remove from the heat, and leave to stand 15 minutes to absorb the flavors.

Discard the onion. Add the bread crumbs to the pan and season to taste. Set the pan over low heat and bring to a boil, stirring constantly. When it begins to boil, remove the pan from the heat and discard the piece of bay leaf. Beat in the butter, one piece at a time, until each piece is thoroughly incorporated. Serve hot.

PAN BAGNA

Pan bagna, or *pan bagnat* as it is sometimes spelled, is the way in which *pain baigné* (meaning "bathed bread") is referred to in the French region of Provence. The essential ingredients are ripe tomatoes, olive oil, and fresh bread; the bread soaks up the juices and become moist. Other ingredients, such as anchovies or artichoke hearts, are added according to preference. *Pan bagna* can be a meal in itself or, in smaller portions, a lunchtime snack.

SERVES 4 AS A MAIN MEAL, 6 TO 8 AS AN APPETIZER

1 long baguette (French loaf)
1¼ pounds ripe tomatoes
½ cup olive oil
1 large garlic clove, crushed
Kosher salt and freshly ground
  black pepper
1½ cups button mushrooms

1 mild white onion
4 ounces canned anchovy fillets
10 ounces artichoke hearts in oil
4 tablespoons chopped fresh
  parsley

Slit the loaf lengthwise without cutting right through; remove all the crumb and reserve.

Scald and peel the tomatoes. Remove and reserve the seeds and juice; cut the flesh into thin strips. Place the tomato flesh in a large bowl. Add half the olive oil and all the garlic and seasonings. Crumble half the reserved crumb of the loaf and mix it into the tomato seeds and juice.

Thinly slice the mushrooms and the onion. Heat the remaining olive oil in a skillet over low heat. Add the onion and cook 5 minutes, or until it is transparent. Add the mushrooms and continue cooking 2 minutes longer, or until they are just cooked through. Remove pan from the heat and leave to cool.

Cut the anchovy fillets in half lengthwise and each half into 2 or 3 pieces crosswise, depending on their size. Drain and slice the artichoke hearts.

Fold the tomato-soaked bread, the mushroom mixture, the anchovies, artichoke hearts, and parsley into the sliced tomato flesh.

Fill the loaf with the mixture and close. Tie the loaf in several places with string to press the sides together and wrap in plastic wrap. Leave the loaf 24 hours in a cool place so the juices soak into the crust.

Serve cut crosswise into portions.

Deep-Fried Breads

In all parts of the world, small pieces of raised dough are deep-fried to make delectable snacks, sweet cakes, or accompaniments to main meals.

In the United States and throughout Europe, the doughnut is perhaps the best-known version of deep-fried bread. The doughnuts we know today probably originated in the Scottish communities living on the borders of northeastern states and Canada in the middle of the nineteenth century. There, these small cakes—crisp on the outside and soft in the middle—were frequently eaten for breakfast, either plain or with maple sugar or maple syrup. Ring doughnuts

Sugared Ring Doughnuts

Makes about 18 doughnuts

½ cup plus 2 tablespoon sugar
1 tablespoon shortening
1 egg, beaten
4 drops vanilla extract
1⅔ cups all-purpose flour
1 teaspoon baking powder
½ teaspoon baking soda
½ teaspoon salt
½ teaspoon ground nutmeg
¾ cup cultured buttermilk (or milk soured with 1 teaspoon cream of tartar)
oil for deep-frying
6 tablespoons superfine sugar

Put the sugar into a large mixing bowl and beat in the shortening. Beat in the egg, a little at a time, and the vanilla extract. Mix the flour with the baking powder, baking soda, salt, and nutmeg. Beat into the sugar mixture, alternately with the buttermilk, to make a very moist dough. Cover the bowl with plastic wrap and put it into the refrigerator at least 1 hour (or overnight if the doughnuts are for breakfast) for the dough to firm.
To shape, put the dough onto a floured work surface and sprinkle with more flour. Roll it to a thickness of about ½ inch. Using a floured 2½-inch round cookie or biscuit cutter, stamp out doughnuts. Stamp out a ½-inch hole in the center of each, again using a floured cutter, or an apple corer. Form the small circles from the middles into a ball again and roll out; repeat until all the dough is used.
Heat a pan of oil over high heat. Sprinkle half the sugar over paper towels. Put the doughnuts into the oil, about 3 at a time. Fry about 1 minute on each side, or until they are golden brown.
Lift them out and place on the paper towels. Sprinkle a little more sugar over the tops. Serve the doughnuts warm.

were the first to become popular. The jam-filled ones were a later development and are now more frequently bought from the bakerery than made at home.

In the cities of Mexico you will find the *churria* or *churro* store, and inside you will be able to buy freshly fried **churros** to accompany a cup of hot chocolate or the milky coffee known as *café con leche*. *Churros* are made from a type of choux pastry dough, which is piped in 7-inch strips into lemon-flavored hot oil and fried until brown and crisp. To serve, they are sprinkled with aniseed-flavored sugar.

Koeksisters are a South African specialty, which are served for dessert or as a sweet snack. White flour, butter, and milk are the main ingredients, together with either yeast or baking powder. The soft dough is made into thin strips which are braided together in threes before being deep-fried. As soon as they are golden and crisp, they are lifted out of the oil and immediately plunged into an ice-cold syrup, flavored with lemon juice and ginger. Once coated in the syrup, they are taken out and left on a wire rack to dry.

Also from South Africa are *vetkoek*, which are eaten as a snack or with meals as a substitute for bread. One version is made simply by deep-frying small pieces of plain white or whole-wheat bread dough until brown and crisp. Quick *vetkoek* are made by dropping spoonfuls of batter into hot oil.

If you are in Trinidad in the Caribbean and want to sample really local food, you will probably be directed to an establishment selling *accra* and "floats." *Accra* are deep-fried fish cakes made with the local salt fish. Floats are the natural accompaniment and are made with a lard or shortening-enriched bread dough, fried in circles which puff up in the oil.

Floats

Makes 10 rolls

1 cake (0.6 oz.) compressed fresh yeast or 1 package active-dry yeast
¾ cup warm water (105° to 115°F)
generous 1 cup cake flour
1 teaspoon salt
4 tablespoons shortening
oil for deep-frying

In a small bowl, sprinkle the yeast into half the water. Leave fresh yeast 5 minutes and dry 15 minutes. Put the flour into a large mixing bowl. Add the salt and cut in the shortening. Make a well in the center. Pour in the yeast liquid and the remaining water. Mix to a dough. Turn the dough onto a floured work surface and knead until it is smooth. Return to the bowl, cover with a clean dish towel, and leave in a warm place 45 minutes, or until it doubles in volume.

Knead the dough again and divide it into 10 small balls. Place them on a floured board or cookie sheet, cover them with a dish towel, and leave 45 minutes longer.

Without kneading again, roll each ball into a round "float," about 3 inches in diameter.

Heat a pan of deep oil over high heat. Put in the "floats," one at a time, and fry about 1 minute on each side until they are golden brown and puffed up. Drain on paper towels. Serve them warm, either as a snack or with a fish dish.

Quick Vetkoek

Makes about 12 small snacks

1⅔ cups white bread flour
½ teaspoon salt
1 tablespoon baking powder
1¼ cups plus 2 tablespoons milk
oil for deep-frying

Put the flour into a mixing bowl. Stir in the salt and baking powder. Make a well in the center and beat in the milk to make a soft batter.

Heat the oil over high heat. Ladle individual tablespoonfuls of the batter into the oil and fry 1 minute on each side, or until they are crisp and golden. Drain the *vetkoek* on paper towels. Serve hot.

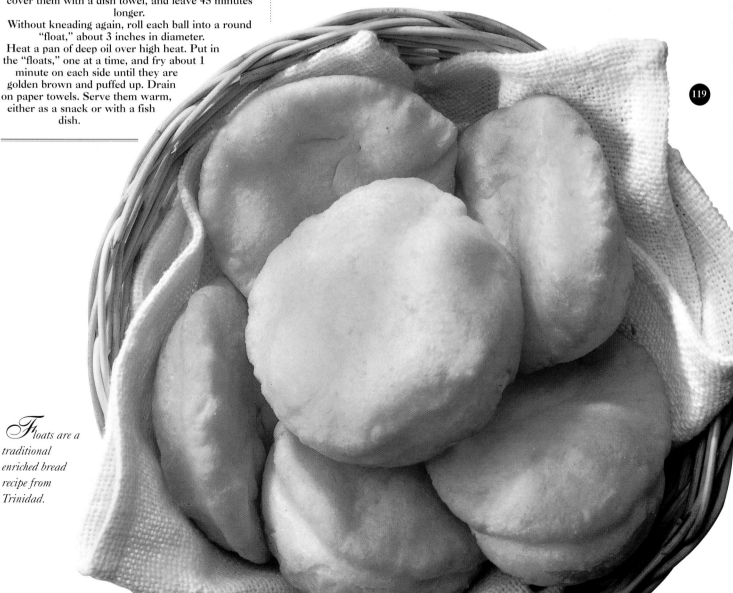

Floats are a traditional enriched bread recipe from Trinidad.

CROSTINI DI MARE

Crostini are pieces of bread brushed with butter or oil and baked until crisp. They can be used as a base for many different kinds of food. In Italy, *Crostini di Mare*, filled with seafood, are a popular snack. As a main meal, serve them with green vegetables or a salad.

SERVES 4

4 slices bread cut from a loaf of Italian bread 2 inches thick
6 tablespoons butter
13 ounces firm white fish
4 ounces fresh, uncooked shelled shrimp

juice of ½ lemon
4 tablespoons chopped fresh parsley

Heat the oven to 400°F. Using a small sharp knife, cut circle about ½ inch in from the crust of each slice of bread, taking the cut to within ½ inch of the bottom. Carefully remove the center crumb, making a bread cup about ½ inch thick. Finely crumble enough of the scooped-out centers to make ½ cup. Melt 4 tablespoons of the butter and use it to brush the bread cups inside and out. Lay them on a cookie sheet. Toast in the oven about 7 minutes, or until they are crisp and golden; keep warm.

Cut the fish into ½-inch cubes. Melt the remaining butter in a large skillet over high heat. Add the fish and shrimp and stir about 2 minutes, or until they are cooked through; remove and keep warm. Add the reserved crumbs to the pan and stir until they turn golden.

Return the fish and shrimp to the pan. Stir in the lemon juice and bring to a simmer. Stir in the parsley. Remove the pan from the heat. Spoon the mixture into the prepared *crostini*. Serve warm.

FRENCH TOAST

Although Americans think of this as a breakfast dish, in other parts of the world it is served as an economical base for sweet and savory snacks. In times of food shortages, French housewives used this recipe as a way of making one egg spread a long way. French toast should be golden and crisp on the outside and light and airy in the middle.

BASIC RECIPE SERVES 4

4 slices medium-cut white bread	*pinch of spice (optional); use*
2 eggs	*different spices for sweet or*
salt and pepper (for savory	*savory serving*
meals only)	*up to 4 tablespoons butter*

Cut the crusts from the bread and cut each slice in half. Beat the eggs in a shallow dish. Add the seasonings, if using. Dip the slices of bread in the beaten egg.

Melt half the butter in a skillet over medium heat. Put in as many slices of bread as the pan will hold and fry about 2 minutes on each side, or until the slices are golden brown and crisp. Cook the remaining pieces of bread in the same way, adding more butter as needed. Serve each slice hot.

Savory Toppings

Serve savory French Toast with baked beans, grated cheese, broiled tomato slices, broiled mushrooms, crispy bacon, sausages, cold meats, vegetable casseroles, mixtures of broiled or roasted vegetables, or salads.

Sweet Toppings

Delicious alternatives include jam or preserves, honey, cinnamon sugar (made by keeping a cinnamon stick in a jar of sugar), vanilla sugar (made by keeping a vanilla bean in a jar of sugar), maple syrup, and stewed fruit or canned or bottled fruit.

LAYERED SMOKED MACKEREL LOAF

Hollowed-out loaves make ideal containers for other ingredients and are perfect for outdoor eating. This one is filled with a simply made smoked mackerel pâté. The ideal loaf for this recipe is one that you have made yourself from the basic bread recipe (page 30) and baked in a 9- x 5- x 2½-inch bread pan. A lot of crumbs result from this filled loaf, which you can use for many of the other recipes in this chapter. Serve the loaf for a lunch or for a special picnic.

SERVES 6

1 white or whole-wheat loaf	*grated peel and juice of 1 lemon*
baked in a 9- x 5- x 2½-inch	*2 tablespoons preserved grated*
bread pan	*horseradish*
2 tablespoons butter	*2 tablespoons tomato paste*
1½ pounds smoked mackerel	*1 teaspoon hot-pepper sauce*
fillets	*1 cup finely chopped fresh*
1½ cups low-fat cream cheese or	*parsley*
fromage blanc	

Slice the rounded top off the loaf. Remove all the inside of the loaf, leaving a shell about ½ inch thick. Butter the inside. Hollow out the top and butter the lower side.

Skin and bone the smoked mackerel fillets; and reserve 6 ounces. Flake the remainder and put them into a bowl; pound with a heavy wooden spoon to break up more. Gradually beat in the cheese and then the lemon peel and juice, horseradish, tomato paste, and hot-pepper sauce. Cut the reserved pieces of mackerel into thin strips.

Put one quarter of the pâté into the bottom of the hollowed loaf. Scatter half the parsley on top in an even layer. Add another quarter of the pâté. Lay all the strips of mackerel on top, running lengthwise along the loaf. Add another quarter of the pâté and top with the remaining parsley. Add the remaining pâté; it should come just above the sides of the loaf. Put on the top and wrap the loaf in plastic wrap.

Refrigerate the loaf 1 hour. Serve cut into slices about 1-inch thick.

Bread-Crumb Stuffing

Different types of bread-crumb stuffing are used around the world for meats, poultry, and vegetables such as sweet bell peppers. The basic recipe is always the same; it is the additions, such as herbs or perhaps small amounts of vegetables, which vary the flavors considerably. Stuffings can be made from white, whole-wheat, or mixed-grain breads, depending on availability and your own personal preferences.

Melt the butter or heat the oil in a skillet over low heat. Add the onion and fry to soften it. With the pan still over the heat, stir in the bread crumbs, the liquid, and the herbs. Season to taste.

If the stuffing is for meat of any kind, cool it completely before using.

BASIC RECIPE SERVES 4 TO 6

*2 tablespoons butter or 4
    tablespoons vegetable oil
1 onion, finely chopped or
    thinly sliced as preferred
2 cups fresh bread crumbs
4 tablespoons liquid (stock, dry
    red or white wine, or cider)*

*1 teaspoon dried or 2
    tablespoons chopped fresh
    herbs
seasoning*

Variations

Herbs

Suggested herb accompaniments include:

With goose and lamb, use 4 chopped sage leaves.

•

With chicken, game, lamb, and turkey, add 1 tablespoon each chopped thyme and marjoram.

•

Lamb is delicious with 1 tablespoon chopped thyme and 1 teaspoon chopped rosemary.

•

Pork works well with 2 chopped sage leaves and 1 teaspoon chopped rosemary needles.

•

Add 2 tablespoons chopped chervil with chicken.

•

With chicken, lamb, and turkey, use 1 tablespoon chopped fresh tarragon.

Vegetables

The following vegetable suggestions should be cooked with the onion in the skillet for the best result:

When cooking lamb, add 1 chopped garlic clove.

•

With game or poultry, add 2 tablespoons chopped or sliced mushrooms for an earthy flavor.

•

For an unusual variation, use ¼ chopped fennel bulb with game, lamb, pork, and poultry.

•

Adding 1 sweet red or green bell pepper, seeded and chopped, goes well with chicken and lamb.

Spices

Add small amounts of the following spices to give a special flavor to the stuffing:

Ground or crushed allspice with chicken, duck, goose, lamb, and pork.

•

Use ground cloves with duck, goose, and lamb.

•

With duck, game, goose, and pork, add crushed juniper berries.

•

Use ground mace to accompany chicken, game, lamb, and turkey.

Nuts

Add small amounts of the following nuts for texture and taste, but beware of any nut allergies:

Try ½ cup chopped walnuts or ½ cup cooked and sliced chestnuts with meat and vegetarian dishes.

•

½ cup chopped brazil nuts is also delicious in most vegetarian dishes.

Fruits

**These fruits add a fresh and interesting flavor
They should be cooked with the onion in the skillet:**

With lamb and pork, add 3 plums, pitted and chopped.

•

Chicken and duck are complemented by adding ½ cup whole red currants.

•

A traditional alternative is to add 1 small cooking apple, peeled, cored, and chopped, with goose and pork.

CHEESE *and* BACON CAKE

This Spanish bread pudding is savory. It originated in La Mancha, a barren plateau in central Spain, and the cheese used locally is made from the milk of the hardy Manchego breed of sheep. The cheese, called *manchego*, is a pressed, uncooked, curd cheese with a slightly salty flavor. If this is not available, feta cheese makes a good substitute. White, thick-sliced bread works best in this recipe. Cheese and Bacon Cake is very rich, and, accompanied by a salad, makes an excellent lunch or supper dish.

Heat the oven to 350°F. Cut the bread into small cubes and put them into the bottom of a 5-cup baking dish. Beat the eggs in a bowl. Beat in the cheese and the milk and season to taste. Pour over the bread.

Stand the pie dish in a baking pan half filled with water. Bake 15 minutes. Place the bacon slices over the top and continue baking 20 minutes longer, or until it is risen and set. Serve sliced either hot or warm.

SERVES 4

4 slices thick-cut white bread	2¼ cups milk
3 eggs	salt and freshly ground black
1 cup crumbled manchego or	pepper
feta cheese	4 slices bacon

PLUM PUDDING

Plum pudding is another medieval dish. Like bread sauce (page 116), it originates from a bread-crumb-based pudding containing dried fruits and spices that was served alongside roast meats. The original pudding had a texture resembling bread sauce, rather than the denser, heavier "cake" of today. This recipe includes whole-wheat bread crumbs, flour, and dark sugar, and is packed with dried fruits. The list of ingredients may look daunting, but the recipe is very easy to make.

SERVES 8

2 ounces whole, dried apricots	4 tablespoons dark brown sugar
½ cup pitted dates	½ cup fresh whole-wheat bread
½ cup currants	crumbs
½ cup raisins	scant ½ cup whole-wheat flour
½ cup golden raisins	¼ cup vegetable suet
½ cup candied peel (in one piece	½ teaspoon baking powder
if possible and chopped just	pinch salt
before using)	¼ nutmeg, grated
⅓ cup dark stout or beer	½ teaspoon ground cinnamon
⅓ cup brandy	1 egg, beaten
2 tablespoons slivered almonds	butter for greasing
1 small cooking apple	

Finely chop the apricots and dates. Put them into a bowl and stir in the currants, raisins, golden raisins, and candied peel. Pour in the stout or beer and the brandy. Cover with a clean dish towel and leave the fruits to soak for 24 hours.

The next day, crush the almond slivers slightly and add to the fruits. Peel and core the apple and grate it into the bowl.

Stir in the sugar, bread crumbs, flour, vegetable suet, baking powder, and salt. Add the spices and beaten egg. Stir everything together and make a wish!

Spoon the mixture into a buttered, 3¾-cup heatproof bowl. Cover the top with a circle of buttered waxed paper and then a circle of foil, both about 2 inches larger than the top of the bowl. Secure both with string and make a handle with a couple of loops for easy lifting.

Place a trivet in the bottom of a large saucepan. Pour in enough water to come about three-quarters up the sides of the bowl when it is standing on the trivet.

Bring the water to a boil and lower in the pudding. Cover the pan tightly and steam the pudding 4 hours, topping up the water with boiling water from the kettle when necessary; do not let the saucepan boil dry.

When ready, lift out the pudding. Remove the paper and foil, leave to cool completely. When cool, replace the 2 coverings and tie on tightly.

On Christmas morning or whenever you plan to serve, steam the pudding in the same way 2 hours longer. Alternatively, you can microwave it for 4 minutes, but remember to remove the foil covering first.

Note: To flame a plum pudding. Just before serving, turn it onto a warmed serving dish. Pour about 3 tablespoons brandy into a ladle and hold the ladle over a candle flame for about 1 minute for the brandy to warm. Light the brandy while it is still in the ladle. Immediately pour it over the pudding where it will burn with a pretty blue flame.

BROWN BREAD *and* HONEY
ICE CREAM

Brown Bread Ice Cream makes a delicious dessert in either summer or winter. It is a simple vanilla ice cream recipe with crunchy bread crumbs caramelized with sugar. The trick is to add the bread crumbs at the last minute and only when the ice cream is almost frozen so they do not soak up too much liquid, and retain their crunch.

MAKES APPROXIMATELY 1 QUART

2 cups fresh whole-wheat bread crumbs	*2¼ cups whole milk*
3 tablespoons sugar	*1 cup plus 2 tablespoons heavy cream*
2 eggs	
2 egg yolks	*1 vanilla bean, or 3 drops vanilla extract*
¼ cup honey	

Heat the oven to 350°F. Place the bread crumbs in a shallow baking pan and scatter the sugar over them. Bake the bread crumbs 5 minutes. Remove the pan, and break up and stir the bread-crumb mixture.

Return the pan to the oven 5 minutes longer until the bread crumbs are golden brown and crisp. Break up the mixture again. Tip it immediately onto a cool, heatproof plate.

Beat the eggs and egg yolks with the honey, either by hand or with an electric mixer, until the mixture is pale and frothy. Pour the milk and cream into a saucepan with the vanilla bean or vanilla extract and bring to just below boiling point. Remove the pan from the heat and remove the vanilla bean, if using. Whip the milk mixture into the egg yolks and honey in a thin, steady stream. Leave the mixture to cool.

Spoon the mixture into a shallow freezerproof container and freeze 3 hours, taking it out every 30 minutes to stir so it freezes evenly. The last time you do this, mix in the bread crumbs.

If you are using an ice cream-maker, follow the manufacturer's directions for vanilla ice cream and add the bread crumbs when the mixture is almost frozen. Leave the ice cream to freeze completely. It can be served immediately or can be packed into a container, covered, and placed in the freezer for storage.

BREAD PUDDING

Bread Pudding is a traditional English dessert that originally was baked for a long time in the slow oven of the kitchen range. It should be light and fluffy in texture and crisp and brown on top. Whole-wheat bread is used in this recipe, but you can also use white bread for a lighter result. An ordinary medium-cut sliced loaf works best.

SERVES 6

3 tablespoons butter, softened	*3 tablespoons sugar*
4 slices medium-cut whole-wheat bread	*freshly grated nutmeg, about ⅛ of a nut*
½ cup raisins	*2 eggs*
½ cup golden raisins	*1 egg yolk*
grated peel of ½ lemon	*2½ cups whole milk*

Heat the oven to 350°F. Butter the bread slices generously and cut them into triangular quarters. In a bowl, mix together the raisins, golden raisins, and lemon peel.

Arrange one-third of the bread slices in the bottom of a 1-quart baking dish. Scatter with half the dried fruit mixture and 1 tablespoon of the sugar. Grate a little nutmeg over. Repeat the layers. Top with the remaining bread slices, the remaining sugar, and remaining grated nutmeg. Beat together the eggs, egg yolk and milk. Pour the egg mixture over the contents of the pan dish.

Stand the pie dish in a baking pan half-filled with water. Bake 30 minutes, or until it is light and risen and the top is golden brown. It is delicious served both warm with custard sauce or ice cream, and cold and sliced.

GENERAL INDEX

127

INDEX *of* RECIPES

CREDITS

Quarto would like to thank the following for providing photographs and
for permission to reproduce copyright material. While every effort has
been made to trace and acknowledge all copyright holders, we would like
to apologize should any omissions have been made.

Key: *t* top, *c* center, *b* below, *r* right, *l* left

ACE Photo Agency 11 *bl* (Keith Eager), 14 *bl* (Paul Thompson); AKG
London 39; Axiom 20 *bl*; e.t.archive 13 *br*; Image Bank 18 *bl*; Image
Select 9 *br*; 21 *br* (Ann Ronan), 57, 17 *tr* (C.F.C.L.), 17; Impact 14 *tr*
(Caroline Penn), 15 *tr* Marcus Pietrek; Life File 7 *tr* (Mike Maidment), 13
tl (Sergei Verein), 87 (Andrew Ward); North Wind Picture Archive 7 *br*, 8
bl, 10 *tl*, 10 *bl*, 11 *tr*, 16 *bl*, 17 *br*, 41, 103; Pictor 16 *tl*; Tony Stone 6, 15 *b*,
66 *b*, 69; Travel Ink 19 (Steve Hines); Visual Arts Library 8 *tl* (Artophot),
18 *tr*, 97, 113 (National Gallery, London. Photo Joseph Martin/VAL).

All other photographs are the copyright of Quarto Publishing plc.

Index by Susan M. Cawthorne